Rob DJ's Monday Night Pub Quiz Book

Michael O'Mara Books Limited

First published in Great Britain in 2009 by
Michael O'Mara Books Limited
9 Lion Yard
Tremadoc Road
London SW4 7NQ

ISBN: 978-1-84317-398-4

1 2 3 4 5 6 7 8 9 10

www.mombooks.com

Cover design by Allan Somerville

Designed and typeset by Burville-Riley Partnership

Printed and bound in Great Britain by CPI Cox & Wyman, Reading, RG1 8EX

Contents

Acknowledgements

This book is dedicated to my wife Tracey, daughters Laura and Jessica, my mum and dad, and all my family and friends.

With special thanks to Chris and Sophie, the breakfast show team Dave, Dom, Carrie, Rachel, Aled, Matt and Piers, and all my friends at Radio 1.

Foreword by Chris Moyles

I have known Rob DJ for far too long now. We met in my local pub in Leeds where he really does do the quiz. (Everything on our radio show is either the truth or based on it.)

I was fascinated by Rob's quiz. The mixture of tough questions and incorrect answers was far too good to be heard only in a northern boozer, so I decided to put it on the air. The idea was that we would repeat some of his quiz questions on the radio the next day. And from that 'Rob DJ's Monday Night Pub Quiz' was born. Many years later, it's still one of my favourite parts of the show. No, really!

Rob is a great mate, a good family man and a terrible drinker. He still refers to London as 'The Smoke' and still has a healthy obsession with Leeds United. He has embarrassed me, annoyed me but above all he has made me laugh. A lot.

I hope you enjoy reading this book and indeed hosting your own quizzes with it. Just please remember that as with Rob's live pub quiz and the radio show version, the answers given in this book may not bear any resemblance to the ACTUAL answers in real life.

Chris Moyles
June 2009

(I put the date in 'cos he may have pissed me off by the time you read this. If so, then I take it all back!)

Introduction: howdy quiz fans!

Well, here we are. Welcome to my quiz book. I'm Rob DJ, the Quizzy Rascal, live from Leeds, England.

So how did I end up getting this gig anyway? Well, I've wanted to be a DJ for as long as I can remember. At just 10 years old I joined the local youth club and was fascinated by the DJ, John. I hung around him to learn the ropes and within two months I was working the decks in the club for all my friends. Gradually I progressed to having my own mobile disco, with dreams of becoming the next Steve Wright and appearing on the greatest radio station in the world – Radio 1.

But it didn't work out quite like that.

On leaving school, I followed a more traditional path and got myself an apprenticeship. At 15, I met my wife-to-be, Tracey, with whom I now have two lovely daughters, Laura and Jessica. Like many people, I put aside my childhood dreams and continued working to provide for my family. And that might have been the end of the story, were it not for the fact that some years later I was approached by a friend and asked to present a 'Disco Quiz' at my local pub.

My local, The Woodman in Leeds, was also that of Vera and Chris Moyles Senior, whose son, having worked through the ranks of local radio, had become a very successful Radio 1 DJ. Chris had achieved everything I had dreamed of as a child. Sharing a love of radio, music, Leeds United and the occasional lager, Chris and I became good friends.

The Woodman is also noted for its open-mic nights, when the pianist Dave invites people up to sing with his trusted compère, MC Mick. One Saturday night I was in the pub with my wife and friends and we were approached to sing – not my forté, but anything for a laugh. At the time, Robbie Williams had recently had a massive number one with 'Rock DJ', and unbeknown to me MC Mick has asked Dave to play this song, changing the lyrics to 'Rob DJ'. The monster was born.

A few years later, Chris and the Breakfast Show team were in town doing the show for a week from Radio Leeds, and they all decided to come to the pub for my Monday Night Quiz. The next morning's Breakfast Show was full of talk of the quiz and the fact that some of the answers may not have been entirely correct. The following Saturday, while chatting to Chris, I offered to email him the quiz for fun, and that's how 'Rob DJ's Monday Night Pub Quiz' began.

Since then my dreams really have been realized. I have presented the quiz live on Radio 1 on Christmas Day (that was very scary), and I was lucky enough to be invited to Radio 1's Big Weekend in Sunderland where we did the quiz live from the Bonded Warehouse. That day my phone was red-hot with text messages from friends and family wishing me well. Just before going on stage, I received another text, this time from Tracey, saying, 'Do you know where the razor blades are as I need to shave my legs?' You can always rely on loved ones to keep you grounded.

Several more invitations to present the quiz followed: live from the Headrow, Leeds with Embrace; live in Leeds with the Kaiser Chiefs; and more recently the Boardmasters event in Newquay, where the crowd joined in with a chant of, 'When I say pub, you say quiz!' While boarding my plane back to Leeds the following day, the check-in assistant asked me for my autograph based on the fact that I was the only Robert on the flight back to Leeds so I must be Rob DJ.

Not to mention my appearance on television quiz show *Eggheads* as captain of the quiz team The Woodentops (the less said about them the better), where I beat Chris Hughes in my head-to-head.

Not bad for an electrician from Leeds with a dream. I would like to thank all my friends and family for their support and help, and I hope you all enjoy this book of brain-teasing questions, even though the answers might not necessarily be right!

Rob DJ, 2009

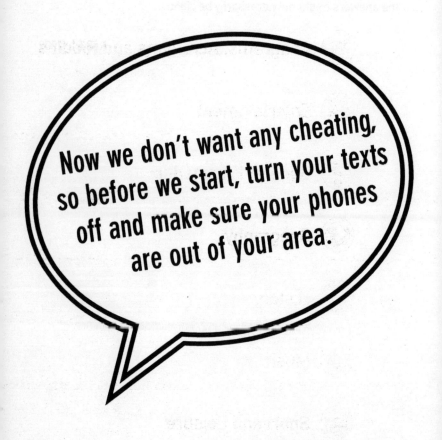

Key to Symbols

(ABC) **Anagrams, Acronyms and Riddles**

(🎬) **Entertainment**

(?) **General Knowledge**

(🌍) **Geography**

(⌛) **History**

(♪) **Music**

(⚽) **Sport and Leisure**

Questions

Howdy quiz fans!
Rob DJ here, live
from Leeds, England,
with another one of
my world-famous
Rob DJ's Monday
Night Pub Quizzes.

QUIZ 1

 1. Who lives at 1600 Pennsylvania Avenue?

 2. What was the capital of Australia before Canberra?

 3. On which London Underground line are West Acton and Shepherds Bush stations?

 4. What was John Lennon's original middle name?

 5. Which animal is listed first in the Oxford English Dictionary?

 6. Which New York DJ had a number-one single in 2001 with 'Another Chance'?

 7. If it is 12 noon in London what time is it in Tokyo, Japan?

 8. Which actor starred alongside Morgan Freeman in the film *Seven*?

 9. Which letters are to the left and right of 'V' on a QWERTY keyboard?

 10. Andy McCluskey was the lead singer of which New Romantic group?

ANSWERS: PAGE 223

11. Against which cricket team did Ian Botham score an unbeaten 148 in 1981 at Headingley?

12. What is the next number in this sequence: 6, 14, 30, 62?

13. Which cult Seventies children's TV character lived at 52 Festive Road?

14. Which country planted its flag on the moon for the first time in 2008?

15. What waterway links Manchester to the Mersey Estuary?

16. Who finished third behind Will Young and Gareth Gates in the original series of *Pop Idol*?

17. In which country would you find the Hanging Gardens of Babylon?

18. Which Beatle was arrested on drugs charges on the same day that Paul McCartney married Linda Eastman?

19. As of 2008, which two premiership sides start and end in the same letter?

20. Which film features All Saints' number-one record 'Pure Shores'?

ANSWERS: PAGE 223

21. Which song became Elvis Presley's first posthumous UK number-one single?

22. In which year did it first become a legal requirement to have a licence for your television?

23. What is the national airline of Holland?

24. What is the name of the TV detective played by David Jason from 1992 to 2009?

25. Which ex-sportsman was sectioned under the Mental Health Act in September 2003?

26. 'BUILT TO STAY FREE' is an apt anagram of which Western landmark?

27. Who had a top-ten UK hit single with the Beatles' 'Got To Get You Into My Life' in 1966?

28. What is the square root of 225?

29. Name the goalkeeper who played for England against Ireland while playing club football in Scotland?

30. Who designed Madonna's famous pointed corset?

ANSWERS: PAGE 223

31. Which disaster took place on 21 December 1988?

 32. Who presents the ITV2 quiz show *Celebrity Juice* with team captains Fearne Cotton and Holly Willoughby?

 33. Which Seventies soul singer died on Independence Day, 2003?

 34. In a 1991 census, which city in the UK had a population of 6,378,600?

 35. In the nursery rhyme, how many blackbirds were baked in a pie?

 36. What might be 12 in London, 10 in New York and 40 in Rome?

 37. What do singers Annie Lennox and Dido have in common?

 38. Who appeared most often at the old Wembley Stadium in its final year of 2000?

 39. In which county is Bishop Auckland?

 40. Born in Hastings in 1961, by what name is Graham McPherson better known?

ANSWERS: PAGE 223

QUIZ 2

 1. On average, how many people travel on the Indian railway system each day?

 2. In which country was Mother Teresa of Calcutta born?

 3. What is the tallest building in Britain?

 4. Who wrote the thriller *Day of the Jackal*?

 5. Who were the last Football League champions before the formation of the Premiership in 1992?

 6. Which Australian band invited Rod Stewart to be the guest vocalist on their 1972 hit 'In A Broken Dream'?

 7. What is the chemical symbol for lead?

 8. What is the largest lake in Italy?

Let's get bizzy with the quizzy

 9. Which city does Arlanda airport serve?

 10. Name the character played by Jennifer Aniston in *Friends*.

ANSWERS: PAGE 223

11. Who became Prime Minister in 1990 following the ousting of Margaret Thatcher?

12. In which city was George Michael arrested for lewd conduct in a public loo?

13. Which is the only English county with no letters in common with the name Lewinsky?

14. Which pop star was the new face or legs of Pretty Polly hosiery in 2003?

15. What was the nickname given to the iconic Beijing National Stadium that staged the 2008 Olympic Games?

16. What is the unit of currency in Cuba?

17. Which former lead singer with Eighties New Romantic band Visage turned his hand to hairdressing in the BBC charity programme *Celebrity Scissorhands*?

18. Which city has an annual Goose Fair?

19. Where would it hurt if you were kicked in the tarsus?

20. What is the sheath from which a hair grows called?

ANSWERS: PAGE 223

21. Which was the last album recorded by The Beatles?

 22. From which club did Manchester United sign Wayne Rooney in 2004 for £25.6 million?

 23. First published in 1864, what is the name of the book that is known as the cricket bible?

 24. Which British railway station has the most platforms?

 25. How is the year 1998 expressed in Roman numerals?

 26. Who became Liverpool manager on 1 December 1959?

 27. Which gospel rap singer had a hit with 'Pray' in 1990?

 28. Which city is served by what was originally called Dum Dum Airport?

 29. Which acid has the chemical formula H_2SO_4?

 30. Which river flows into the sea at Plymouth?

ANSWERS: PAGE 223

31. Which was the first James Bond movie of the 1980s?

 32. What was Europe's tallest building when the Queen declared it officially open in 1981?

 33. In which film did the wind from the subway blow up Marilyn Monroe's dress?

 34. Which group had a hit with 'Substitute' in 1978?

 35. Which two boxers took part in the so-called 'Rumble in the Jungle' in Zaire in 1976?

 36. Who was the Maid of Orleans?

 37. Who won his first Formula One World Championship race at Spa in Belgium in 1992?

 38. Who was Australian Prime Minister from 1996 to 2007?

 39. Which bird has the longest wingspan?

 40. Who played the character of Dorothy Michael in the Eighties movie *Tootsie*?

ANSWERS: PAGE 223

QUIZ 3

1. Whose portrait appears on the back of a £50 note?

2. What was the name of Dennis the Menace's dog?

3. Which Geordie was voted PFA Young Player of the Year in 1988?

4. Which group had a hit with 'Hang On Sloopy' in 1965?

5. What is the state capital of California?

6. Who makes perfume called Obsession and aftershave called Escape for Men?

7. Which musical set in New York's slums is based on Shakespeare's *Romeo and Juliet*?

8. Which breed of dog has the best eyesight?

9. What is the highest hand in 3-card Brag?

10. On which island was Napoleon born?

ANSWERS: PAGE 224

11. Which cosmetic company's products are known as 'the make-up of make-up artists'?

 12. Which duo had a 1992 UK number-one hit with 'Would I Lie To You'?

 13. What increased to 12 hours a day in 1988 for the first time since 1914?

 14. David Sneddon won the first series of *Fame Academy*, but who won the second series?

 15. Who took 73 wickets and scored 3,816 runs for Middlesex in 1947?

 16. What is the longest river in Italy?

 17. From what drug is crack derived?

 18. What is the designer label DKNY an abbreviation for?

 19. How many seconds are there in a week?

 20. Colombo is the capital of which Commonwealth country?

ANSWERS: PAGE 224

21. Which comedy duo lived on Oil Drum Lane?

 22. From which country did Finland declare independence in 1917?

 23. Which skirt takes its name from a writing implement?

 24. Which two letters are worth ten points in *Scrabble*?

 25. Who made the first sound recording on 6 December 1877?

 26. Which famous horse won the Cheltenham Gold Cup in 1989?

 27. In which street would you find the Bank of England?

 28. Which former President of the Soviet Union died in 1953 aged 73?

 29. Which international spirit is made on the island of Barbados?

 30. Whose 1992 autobiography was entitled *What's it all About*?

ANSWERS: PAGE 224

31. In golf, which club is used on the green?

 32. In the summer of which year did the Battle of Britain take place?

 33. What was the name of Frankie Valli's backing group?

 34. Who owned the factory in the Roald Dahl book *Charlie and the Chocolate Factory*?

 35. Who discovered penicillin in 1928?

 36. By what name is a young kangaroo known?

 37. Which country hosted the Rugby Union World Cup in 1999?

 38. Where would you find the BBC's main radio transmitter serving Yorkshire and Lancashire?

 39. What is the capital of the Philippines?

 40. Who released a version of Depeche Mode's 1981 hit 'Just Can't Get Enough' for Comic Relief in 2009?

ANSWERS: PAGE 224

QUIZ 4

 1. Which mountain overlooks Cape Town in South Africa?

 2. What item of clothing is a 'farthingale'?

 3. Which member of The Beatles was born at 12 Arnold Grove, Liverpool?

 4. What licence cost 37p when it was abolished in 1988?

 5. In slang, how much money is a 'monkey'?

 6. In which British town did Michael Ryan run riot, killing 14 people?

 7. Which radio presenter gave birth to her first child Rudy Brae on 10 June 2008?

 8. What did Mary Phelps Jacob invent in 1913?

 9. In which British seaside resort was the TV sitcom *Fawlty Towers* set?

 10. From which country do the Gurkhas come from?

ANSWERS: PAGE 224

11. Which group were 'zipping up my boots, going back to my roots' in 1981?

 12. In which country was Adolf Hitler born?

 13. Which 1969 film was remade in 2003 starring Mark Wahlberg?

 14. Which company makes the perfume Flower?

 15. Which banknote did the Bank of England introduce in 1752 and withdraw in 1945?

 16. What is a self-contained underwater breathing apparatus better known as?

 17. Who was the second wife of Henry VIII?

 18. Which is the world's most populous city?

 19. What was name of the film that used 300,000 extras in just one scene?

 20. Who left Take That in July 1995?

ANSWERS: PAGE 224

21. What toy was voted the most popular of the 20th century?

 22. Was the Battle of Jutland a land, sea or air battle?

 23. Name the two countries that start but do not end with the letter 'A'.

 24. Who invented the world's first 'bagless' vacuum cleaner?

 25. Which animal is the fastest on earth?

 26. What was the name of Kate Bush's 1978 number-one record, inspired by an Emily Brontë novel?

 27. Which London restaurant opened in 1989 with Sgt Pepper Steak and Penny Lane Pâté on the menu?

 28. Which city is furthest east: Athens, Budapest or Helsinki?

 29. Which liquid chemical is mixed with powder bleach to dye hair blonde?

 30. Which Sheffield band's hits included 'Disco 2000' and 'Common People'?

ANSWERS: PAGE 224

31. Who caused David Beckham to visit hospital in need of stitches in February 2003?

 32. Who formed Microsoft with his school friend Paul Allen?

 33. Which city is served by Schiphol Airport?

 34. In snooker, what colour ball is worth 4 points?

 35. Who played the character Buffy Summers in the TV series *Buffy the Vampire Slayer*?

 36. How many TT Races did Mike Hailwood win in his career?

 37. What is 60 per cent of 260?

 Don't forget, we're now under strict exam conditions

 38. What began on 14 July 1789?

 39. What was the name of the woodpecker on the children's TV programme *Bagpuss*?

 40. Which is the biggest country in the world by area?

ANSWERS: PAGE 224

QUIZ 5

1. Katie White is the lead singer of which band from Leigh, Greater Manchester?

2. Which boxer had the most title fights in his career?

3. In which city was John F. Kennedy assassinated?

4. Which country would you associate with ciabatta bread?

5. Who was Superman's girlfriend?

6. What does a toxicologist study?

7. What is the capital of Alaska?

8. Which female singer had a hit in 1959 with 'Lipstick On Your Collar'?

9. What number was PC McGarry in the children's TV programme *Camberwick Green*?

10. Who was the leader of the Labour Party before Tony Blair?

ANSWERS: PAGE 225

11. What does DVD stand for?

 12. What did Wallace H. Carothers invent in 1937?

 13. For which film did Donna Summer record the song 'Down Deep Inside' in 1977?

 14. Which two British ex-Prime Ministers are mentioned in the Beatles' record 'Taxman'?

 15. What is a narwhal?

 16. Which spy plane was shot down over Russia in 1960?

 17. What would you be if you were dextral?

 18. If Monday's child is fair of face, what is Wednesday's child?

 19. Which is the busiest passenger airport in the world?

 20. How many gold medals did Team GB win at the Beijing Olympics?

ANSWERS: PAGE 225

21. In what castle would you find the Scottish Crown Jewels?

 22. 'Nobody puts Baby in a corner' is a classic line from which 1987 film?

 23. What nickname was given to the Iraqi Minister of Information during the Iraq War?

 24. In which county is Ipswich?

 25. Which football club play their home games at Sincil Bank?

 26. Which former member of the Housemartins became Fat Boy Slim?

 27. Which former Chief Executive of the FA is now the Chief Executive of Royal Mail?

 28. How many hours is Moscow ahead of GMT?

 29. How many sides does a prism usually have?

 30. Which ex-member of The Rolling Stones had a 1981 hit with 'Je Suis Un Rockstar'?

ANSWERS: PAGE 225

31. Who did President John F. Kennedy's widow marry in 1968?

32. Which French word for 'boost' is worn to enhance a women's figure?

33. Which is the largest city south of the equator?

34. From where in London was the first British television broadcast made?

35. What was the name of the computerized pop music TV presenter on Channel Four in the Eighties?

36. Who lived at 25 Cromwell Street, Gloucester?

37. Which ex-Rat Pack member had a hit with 'Gentle On My Mind' in 1969?

38. What gift is traditionally given to celebrate a tenth wedding anniversary?

39. What was the name of the robbers' farmhouse hideout following the Great Train Robbery in 1963?

40. What does the queen hold in her hand in a standard pack of cards?

ANSWERS: PAGE 225

QUIZ 6

 1. Who designed the Clifton Suspension Bridge in Bristol, which opened in 1864?

 2. In which decade did Barbie first appear?

 3. Who wrote the 1990 book *Silence of the Lambs*?

 4. Which classic 1966 Beach Boys album featured 'Wouldn't It Be Nice' and 'God Only Knows'?

 5. In 1967, what was the first British club to win the European Cup?

 6. Who played Bluebottle in *The Goon Show*?

 7. What is Kylie Minogue's lingerie range called?

 8. What was the name of the New York club made famous for breaking the punk scene with Blondie and The Ramones?

 9. Which queen ordered the creation of a racecourse at Ascot in 1711?

 10. Which Australian city stands on the Swan River?

ANSWERS: PAGE 226

11. What was the name of Michael J. Fox's character in the *Back to the Future* trilogy?

 12. What is a larnax?

 13. The name of which musical instrument comes from the Greek words for 'wood' and 'voice'?

 14. What in New Zealand is a ricker: a bird, a fish or a tree?

 15. How long does it take, to the nearest hour, for the moon to complete a full cycle from new moon to new moon?

 16. What is the name of Ireland's national airline?

 17. Which is Florida's largest 'key'?

 18. What name is given to a dish of chicken, bacon and red wine?

 19. Name the comedian Paul O'Grady's drag alter ego.

 20. What is 65 per cent of 2,500?

ANSWERS: PAGE 226

21. Buster Bloodvessel was the lead singer of which ska band?

 22. What did the acronym *Tiswas* stand for?

 23. What is measured by an altimeter?

 24. What was the nationality of the referee in the 1966 World Cup final?

 25. Why did Aaron Barschak make all the front pages of the papers in June 2003?

 26. Name the two New York boroughs that begin with the letter B.

 27. Tina O'Brien played which character in *Coronation Street*?

 28. Which is the world's most southerly capital city?

 29. What is a hammerkop: a bird, a fish or a tree?

 30. What is the main ingredient of nail polish remover?

ANSWERS: PAGE 226

31. What name is given to the tendons at the back of the knee?

 32. According to The Beatles' song 'A Day in the Life' how many holes were found in Blackburn, Lancashire?

 33. Which Fifties crooner who had a hit with 'Do You Mind' was married to Joan Collins from 1963 to 1970?

 34. What name is given to a cocktail consisting of vodka and orange?

 35. In which town did Billy Butlin open his first holiday camp in 1936?

 36. Name the only footballer to have played in the Manchester, Merseyside and Glasgow derbies.

 37. What is the collective term given to the colours red, yellow and blue?

 38. Which two cities are joined by Route 66?

 39. Who was the lead singer of Cockney Rebel?

 40. What would you be doing if you were using a swedge?

ANSWERS: PAGE 226

QUIZ 7

 1. James T. Kirk was the captain of the Starship Enterprise, but what does the 'T' stand for?

 2. What is the capital of Hong Kong?

 3. What name is given to the shortest of all miniskirts?

 4. Which Dutch artist was born in 1853?

 5. Who was the 43rd President of the United States of America?

 6. What was the boat called in the film *Jaws*?

Just say what you see

 7. In which city was Dick Turpin hanged?

 8. In which year did the Great Potato Famine begin in Ireland?

 9. Who, on 30 October 1961, was moved from his tomb in Red Square?

 10. Who scored England's only try in the 2003 Rugby World Cup Final win?

ANSWERS: PAGE 227

11. Which member of Destiny's Child starred in the Austin Powers film *Goldmember*?

 12. In which county is the market town of Devizes?

 13. Who covered Tears for Fears' 1982 hit 'Mad World', becoming Christmas number one in 2003?

 14. In computer terms, how many bits are there in a byte?

 15. Which of Disney's seven dwarves is last alphabetically?

 16. What is the common name of sodium hydroxide?

 17. Which supermodel was formerly married to Richard Gere?

 18. Which country hosted the 1998 football World Cup?

 19. In *The Simpsons*, what is the supermarket run by Apu called?

 20. What weapon did Robert Whitehead invent in 1866?

ANSWERS: PAGE 227

21. If you throw a pair of dice and add the numbers, which score comes up most often?

 22. Which DJ got his big break standing in for Kenny Everett when he was off work sick?

 23. Johnny Fingers was the pop pianist with which group?

 24. Name the detective played by Jodie Foster in the film *Silence of the Lambs*.

 25. In which US state does the original London Bridge now stand?

 26. What was the name of the annual fashion show that first took place at the Royal Albert Hall in October 2003 featuring live pop acts for the Prince's Trust?

 27. Where would you find the Spanish Steps?

 28. What was the name of the first Prime Minister of England in 1721?

 29. What was the name of Take That's comeback album in 2006?

 30. Which two cities are joined by the M62?

ANSWERS: PAGE 227

31. Name the comedian who has adapted Rod Stewart's life story for the theatre?

 32. At 2,648 feet, which waterfall in Venezuela is the world's longest waterfall?

 33. Who was the second man to set foot on the moon in 1969 after Neil Armstrong?

 34. Which is the longest river in Great Britain?

 35. What colour is motor racing's caution flag?

 36. Which British airport carries the most chartered or holiday flights?

 37. Before decimalization how many pence were there in a pound sterling?

 38. What physical characteristic do supermodels Niki Taylor and Cindy Crawford share?

 39. Which Eighties duo were given a Lifetime Achievement Award at the 2009 BRIT Awards?

 40. What nationality was the actor Boris Karloff?

ANSWERS: PAGE 227

QUIZ 8

1. What is the only anagram of the word 'Monday'?

2. What did Frank Hornby patent in 1901?

3. What number is on the back of the shirt that David Beckham wears for AC Milan?

4. What is the only fruit to have seeds on the outside?

5. What part of the body is also the name of a punctuation mark?

6. Which is the only vowel on a standard keyboard that is not on the top row of letters?

7. What was the name of Eddie Murphy's character in the *Beverly Hills Cop* films?

8. How many stars are on the European Union Flag?

9. In which city in England is the National Railway Museum?

10. In the 1963 film *The Great Escape*, what names were given to the three tunnels?

ANSWERS: PAGE 227

11. 'I can run, but I can't walk. I've got a mouth, but I can't talk. I have a head, but I never weep. I have a bed, but I never sleep.' What am I?

12. Which group needed 'somebody to love' in 2004?

13. Which film directed by Danny Boyle won 4 Golden Globes, 7 BAFTAs and 8 Oscars in 2009?

14. What are dried plums called?

15. In which city was Martin Luther King assassinated in 1968?

16. Which British prison was the scene of a major riot on April Fool's Day in 1990?

17. What name is given to someone who does not eat any food of animal origin?

18. Name the six colours on a standard Rubik's cube.

19. What is Britain's largest lake?

20. From which country do French fries originate: France, Belgium or Switzerland?

ANSWERS: PAGE 227

21. Who was the lead singer of the Commodores before having an extremely successful solo career?

 22. What is the policeman's name in the *Noddy* stories?

 23. What is the alternative common name for a black leopard?

 24. Which mountain overlooks Rio de Janeiro?

 25. Which number is the odd one out: 3, 13, 23, or 33?

 26. What colour are the seats in the House of Lords: red, blue or green?

 27. What is the largest country in Africa?

 28. In 1931, what became the first ever televized sports event?

 29. In which movement would you find a Brown Owl as leader?

 30. Paraguay and which other country are the only landlocked nations in South America?

ANSWERS: PAGE 227

31. Which ex-*Blue Peter* presenter has a pop-star daughter called Sophie?

32. Which US President once worked as a fashion model: Gerald Ford or Ronald Reagan?

33. Which English king forced the dissolution of the monasteries in 1536?

34. How many counters does each player have at the start of a game of Backgammon?

35. Which famous British ship's name means 'the short skirt'?

36. 'REVENGE IS OUR WAY' is an anagram of the name of which Hollywood actress? (2 words)

37. Which female singer has had more UK top-ten singles than the Rolling Stones and The Beatles combined?

38. What is the sum of degrees in the internal angles of a triangle?

39. Who in 1945 became the first president of Vietnam until his death in 1969?

40. In which sport is the Thomas Cup a major prize?

ANSWERS: PAGE 227

QUIZ 9

1. Where did Robbie Williams have three sell-out concerts in the summer of 2003?

2. What country has the largest area under vine?

3. Which mammal can jump the highest?

4. What was the name of *Hong Kong Phooey*?

5. Who had a hit with 'It's A Man's World' in 1966?

6. Minsk is the capital of which country?

Pens ready, papers steady, let's quiz!

7. Who was born at 20 Forthlin Road, Liverpool in June 1942?

8. Which is the bestselling car of all time?

9. Which island is the most easterly of the West Indies?

10. Carrots are rich in which vitamin?

ANSWERS: PAGE 228

11. What programme topped the British TV ratings every year from 1979 to 1989?

 12. What colour is the cross on the Swiss flag?

 13. Which London Underground line would you be on if you travelled direct from Camden Town to London Bridge?

 14. What is the unit of currency in Bulgaria?

 15. Which singer/actress starred in the title role of the 1953 film *Calamity Jane*?

 16. Which song on The Beatles' *Sgt Pepper's Lonely Hearts Club Band* ends with a chord sustained for forty seconds?

 17. American film director D. W. Griffith invented which popular female accessory?

 18. Donald Neilson was better known as which notorious 1970's murderer?

 19. Which golfer died on 26 October 1999 in a freak Learjet crash?

 20. Which is the largest of the Great Lakes?

ANSWERS: PAGE 228

21. Who had the bestselling single of 1981 with 'Tainted Love'?

 22. Which actor, who died in January 2008, played roles as diverse as Ned Kelly, Casanova and Bob Dylan?

 23. What is the collective name for a group of penguins?

 24. Which city gave its name to Frankie Goes to Hollywood's second album?

 25. What product would you associate Manolo Blahnik with?

 26. What is the capital of Pakistan?

 27. Which event pulled the world's biggest TV audience on 13 July 1985?

 28. On which river does Dublin stand?

 29. Which group were living in a 'Banana Republic' in 1979?

 30. Which disease caused the deaths of 43 people in Croydon in 1937?

ANSWERS: PAGE 228

31. Which of Disney's seven dwarfs wears glasses?

 32. What colour is the Golden Gate Bridge?

 33. Of which flower family is the apple a member?

 34. What is the Italian word for 'coast'?

 35. Mother Teresa was famous for her work among the poor of which city?

 36. Designer John Galliano makes clothes for which international fashion house?

 37. Which English city exports cutlery all over the world?

 38. Which British soul group had hits in the Sixties with 'Build Me Up Buttercup' and 'Baby Now That I've Found You'?

 39. Which is the smallest county in England?

 40. On what day of the week did World War Two begin: Friday, Saturday, or Sunday?

ANSWERS: PAGE 228

QUIZ 10

 1. What first appeared in 1969 and retired from service in 2003?

 2. Which species is the largest of the bear family?

 3. Which Eighties children's TV cartoon featured the voices of David Jason and Terry Scott?

 4. In engine terms, what is OHC an abbreviation for?

 5. Who was born David Robert Jones in London 1947?

 6. According to the advertising slogan, 'Maybe she's born with it', or maybe it's what?

 7. Which is the world's longest mountain range?

 8. Which is London's most frequently stolen street sign?

 9. Which actor and teen idol died in a car crash on 30 September 1955?

 10. Which British city has more canals than Venice?

ANSWERS: PAGE 228

11. In which year was the former British colony of Hong Kong returned to China?

 12. In which year was the last ever episode of *Coronation Street* transmitted in black and white?

 13. In which country would you visit the Great Slave Lake?

 14. How many sides has a dodecagon?

 15. Which darts player is known as 'The Power'?

 16. Who is tennis player Andre Agassi married to?

 17. In which cartoon would you find Elmer Fudd?

 18. Who makes the perfume Baby Doll?

 19. Paul 'Bonehead' Arthurs was the founder member of which group?

 20. Which British army regiment is known as the Sappers?

ANSWERS: PAGE 228

21. On which river does Cardiff stand?

 22. In which US state is Chicago?

 23. Which has more protein: a chicken or a bag of nuts?

 24. Which club have won Rugby League's Challenge Cup the most times with 17 wins?

 25. Which is furthest west: London or Edinburgh?

 26. What was the name of the rogue trader who took Barings Bank down in February 1995?

 27. What is the minimum allowed age of a horse in steeplechasing?

 28. Who sang of a 'dedicated follower of fashion' in 1966?

 29. Which fruit has no rhyme?

 30. Who was voted the leader of the British suffragette movement in 1906?

ANSWERS: PAGE 228

31. What does the acronym DERV stand for?

 32. Which is the third planet from the sun?

 33. What is the medical name for German measles?

 34. Who won the BBC Sports Personality of the Year in 2003?

 35. In which county is Reading?

 36. Which waterway links the Mediterranean Sea to the Red Sea?

 37. What was the name of the contestant who coughed the answers to Major Ingram on *Who Wants to be a Millionaire*?

 38. What was the name of the space shuttle that blew up on re-entry in February 2003?

 39. Where was Saddam Hussein found hiding in a cellar: Tikrit, Kirkuk or Baghdad?

 40. In the 2008 US election campaign who was chosen as John McCain's running mate?

ANSWERS: PAGE 228

QUIZ 11

 1. What was the bestselling album of 2003 in the UK?

 2. Which African dictator seized control of Uganda in 1971?

 3. Which former British Prime Minister's partner passed away in 2003?

 4. Which was the first British ship to sink in the Falkland's war?

 5. Which 2008 film became the highest-grossing film in Britain of all time?

 6. Which Beatles song did Cherie Blair sing to students on a visit to China?

 7. Arnold Schwarzenegger is Governor of which US state?

 8. Which three digits have prefixed all directory enquiries provider numbers since 2003?

 9. Which illusionist lost nearly four stone in 44 days living in a glass box on the banks of the River Thames?

 10. Which England footballer admitted losing £30,000 playing cards at the 2002 World Cup?

ANSWERS: PAGE 229

11. Which city was capital of the USA before it became Washington D.C. in 1800?

 12. In the film *Bambi* what type of animal is Thumper?

 13. Who invented the telephone?

 14. Which indie band from Eastbourne had hits with 'Achilles Heel' and 'Dancing In The Moonlight'?

 15. Which football club play their home games at the Hawthornes?

 16. Whose own-brand cosmetics range is called No 7?

 17. What is pontoon called when played in a casino?

 18. Which bestselling tabloid newspaper was launched in 1964?

 19. Where in Paris is the tomb of the Unknown Soldier?

 20. Marble Arch was originally built as part of Buckingham Palace: true or false?

ANSWERS: PAGE 229

21. What do adult humans have 206 of?

 22. Prior to Lewis Hamilton, which Scot became the world's youngest Formula One World Champion in 1963?

 23. If you were born on 22 June what star sign would you be?

 24. What did US President Barack Obama promise his daughters during his victory speech?

 25. What type of clothing are culottes?

 26. The origin of the banana can be traced back to which continent: Asia, Africa or South America?

 27. What dance craze did punks introduce?

 28. In 1972 Britain joined the EEC with Denmark and which other country?

 29. Which monarch died in 1837 leaving Queen Victoria to take the throne?

 30. What does the abbreviation DAT stand for?

ANSWERS: PAGE 229

31. What is the state capital of Maine?

32. On what part of the body are deely boppers worn?

33. Which Scottish bridge was opened by Queen Elizabeth in 1964?

34. Which duo had a hit with 'Solid' in 1984?

35. Where did the Muffin Man live?

36. Who became the youngest President of the USSR in 1985?

37. What planet came within 34.6 million miles of earth in 2003?

38. Which ex-Arsenal player became the face of Renault Clio?

39. Which country covers 3,695,000 square miles?

40. Who was axed from his morning show following alleged racist comments in 2004?

ANSWERS: PAGE 229

QUIZ 12

 1. Where on your body would you get a stye?

 2. What was the name of the hanged A6 murderer who was exhumed in 2001?

 3. Which band's rhythm guitarist Richey Edwards mysteriously vanished on 1 February 1995?

 4. Middlesbrough plays its home games at the Riverside Stadium, but what is the name of its previous ground?

 5. If you arrived at Waverley Station which city would you be in?

 6. Which horse came second to Red Rum in the 1973 Grand National?

 7. What does PTO mean on the bottom of a letter?

 8. At 45 miles, which is the longest river in Yorkshire?

 9. What is the maximum number of clubs a golfer can take onto the course?

 10. What is the name for a female fox?

ANSWERS: PAGE 230

11. It first became legal to sell what in the Irish Republic in 1985?

 12. Which company advertise their products with the slogan 'Because I'm worth it'?

 13. Why was Bogdale in Kent in the news on 10 August 2003?

 14. What was the name of the character played by Michael Clarke Duncan in the film *The Green Mile*?

 15. Who discovered the island of Cuba?

 16. What did Minh Thai solve in a record 26 seconds in 1981?

 17. What was the name of the record by Tommy Roe that was covered by comedian Vic Reeves and The Wonder Stuff?

 18. Whose plane is Air Force One?

 19. Who was the voice of Rugby League until his death in 1986?

 20. In which war was the Charge of the Light Brigade?

ANSWERS: PAGE 230

21. What is the state capital of Texas?

 22. What sort of tree did George Washington reputedly cut down?

 23. On which Greek island would you find the resort of Faliraki?

 24. What was Robbie Williams's first solo UK number one?

 25. What is the national airline of Australia?

 26. Who is the patron saint of England?

 27. Who won his third successive World Snooker Championship in 1989?

 28. Which comedian made the bestselling DVD in the UK of 2003?

 29. What was raised to £175,000 for a period of one year from 3 September 2008?

 30. Who followed George VI to the throne?

ANSWERS: PAGE 230

31. Which political party had its headquarters in Walworth Road, London until 1997?

 32. Which US city is known as the home of Motown Records?

 33. Which industrialist became the world's first billionaire in 1909?

 34. What is the name of the police officer in the cartoon series *Top Cat*?

 35. What is the national airline of Hong Kong?

 36. If every batsman in a cricket team is bowled out first bowl, how many players are not?

 37. Which American rocker is known as 'The Boss'?

 38. Which painter is famous for his pictures of matchstick men?

 39. Which Stanley Kubrick film was set in Vietnam but filmed in London's Docklands?

 40. What was the name of the chocolate bar advertised by Terry Scott dressed as a schoolboy?

ANSWERS: PAGE 230

QUIZ 13

 1. In which year did Tony Blair become Prime Minister?

 2. Which record company turned down The Beatles but signed The Rolling Stones?

 3. What do chefs refer to as 'the master spice'?

 4. Who did the Germans defeat in the battle of Tannenberg in 1914?

 5. What worked wonders, according to the 1970s advertising campaign?

 6. Which river runs through the Grand Canyon?

 7. To which plant family does the raspberry belong?

 8. Which pop star died on 16 September 1977?

 9. What is the state capital of Tennessee?

 10. How many members were there in the Walton family?

ANSWERS: PAGE 231

11. Which England defender punched the ball off the line to give away a penalty in the 1966 World Cup semi-final against Portugal?

12. What does the O stand for in the term O Level?

13. Helen Sharman was famous for being the first Britain to go where?

14. Name the short, layered skirt worn to discos in the 1980s.

15. What does the term SWAT stand for in the US police force?

16. How many different letters are used in roman numerals?

17. Which ex-Liverpool and Tottenham footballer starred in *I'm a Celebrity … Get Me Out of Here*?

18. What was George Michael's first number one?

19. What does the 'e' in e-mail stand for?

20. What gambling implements are known as 'devil's bones'?

ANSWERS: PAGE 231

21. What is the name of Tintin's dog?

Schnizzle my quizzle

22. What is a linden tree also known as?

23. Who said 'If you can't stand the heat, get out of the kitchen'?

24. What fast food was originally advertised as being 'Finger Lickin' Good'?

25. Who married John Major's son in 1999?

26. What is the name of the fluid secreted by the liver?

27. Which Eighties group had a lead singer called Robert Bell?

28. Which company invented the Walkman?

29. Who won the Irish Peace Prize in 2000?

30. What product were you encouraged to apply to the carpet to 'put the freshness back'?

ANSWERS: PAGE 231

31. Into which sea does the River Jordan flow?

 32. What is the state capital of Utah?

 33. Which is the longest ring road in the world at 121 miles long?

 34. Which Rugby Union team play their home games at Edgeley Park?

 35. 'Frog and toad' is Cockney rhyming slang for what?

 36. In a court of law, what name is given to the area where the accused sits?

 37. What is the weakest piece in a game of chess?

 38. Which group from Wigan had a number-one album called *Urban Hymns*?

 39. What are the seaside resorts of Torquay, Paignton and Brixham collectively known as?

 40. What does a hygrometer measure?

QUIZ 14

 1. Which river does Amsterdam stand on?

 2. Which plant is the symbol of Ireland?

 3. In which fictional town is the TV programme *Home and Away* set?

 4. What do the zodiac signs Leo, Aries and Sagittarius have in common?

 5. What is Au the chemical symbol for?

 6. Which 2003 summer number-one single for Beyoncé Knowles became the best selling ringtone of the year?

 7. What type of animal is a natterjack?

 8. Which Seventies sweet carried the slogan 'A man's gotta chew what a man's gotta chew'?

 9. What animal is the nickname of Millwall Football Club?

 10. Which company co-invented the compact disc with Sony?

ANSWERS: PAGE 231

11. Which television programme features the Gallagher family?

 12. In which American state is the Hoover Dam?

 13. What four-letter word is a unit of electrical power?

 14. Which two brothers played the Krays in the 1990 film of that name?

 15. Which county is nicknamed the 'Garden of England'?

 16. Which lingerie company originally made the Wonderbra?

 17. Susanne Sully and Joanne Catherall were the female vocalists with which Eighties group?

 18. What is the capital of Trinidad and Tobago?

 19. What was the 'Chopper' bicycle's smaller brother?

 20. What fruit gave the name to the lead character in the film *The Third Man*?

ANSWERS: PAGE 231

21. What types of clouds produce rain or snow?

 22. What is origami the art of?

 23. In which city would you find the Borodinsky Bridge?

 24. Who exposed herself to international TV viewers during the 2004 Super Bowl half-time entertainment?

 25. What happened to the *Mona Lisa* on 21 August 1911?

 26. In which fictional part of London is the TV programme *EastEnders* set?

 27. What did Edward Lowe invent: power steering, air conditioning or cat litter?

 28. Which transport provider gave The Divine Comedy a top-ten hit single in 1999?

 29. What is longer, a yard or a metre?

 30. How many periods are there in a hockey game: 2, 3, 4 or 5?

ANSWERS: PAGE 231

31. In the nursery rhyme, who asked for his 'fiddlers three'?

 32. What US state is called the 'Bullion State'?

 33. Before Tiger Woods, who was the last golf professional to win at least five tournaments in a row?

 34. What chocolate bar, launched in 1866, is the oldest in England?

 35. What is a human's largest internal organ?

 36. Which is the largest planet in the solar system?

 37. What is the traditional colour of a fez?

 38. Where did race riots start on 11 April 1981?

 39. What was murderer John George Haigh's infamous nickname?

 40. What is the capital of the Czech Republic?

ANSWERS: PAGE 231

QUIZ 15

 1. What is the name of the *Heartbeat* spin-off series set in a hospital?

 2. 'You never close your eyes any more when I kiss your lips' are the opening lyrics to which classic song?

 3. What is a Molotov cocktail?

 4. What cocktail contains Malibu, Blue Curaçao and pineapple juice?

 5. Which ex-England cricket all-rounder also played football for Scunthorpe?

 6. Which two metals make the alloy brass?

 7. Which football club play their home games at the Kingston Communication Stadium?

 8. In which city would you find the George Washington Bridge?

 9. Who designed and built the first internal combustion automobile?

 10. Who is Katie Price better known as?

ANSWERS: PAGE 232

11. Where in 1896 did the first modern Olympic Games take place?

 12. Which group released an album called *Live in Leeds*?

 13. Which cosmetics guru was born Florence Nightingale Graham?

 14. What US state is called the Sunshine State?

 15. Which Eighties arcade game was invented by computer programmer Toru Iwatani, who was inspired when he saw a pizza with one slice missing?

 16. Which country has the longest coastline?

 17. Which company manufactures Max Factor cosmetics?

 18. Which king of England was forced to abdicate in 1399?

 19. What was originally classified as the smallest planet in the Solar System?

 20. Which Paris club is famous for the cancan?

ANSWERS: PAGE 232

21. Why is there one star on the England football shirt?

 22. Which country declared war on Britain and France in June 1940?

 23. Which sea is furthest north: Black, White or Red?

 24. What name is shared by the infertile offspring of animals of different species and a strapless ladies' shoe?

 25. What is the capital of Hungary?

 26. Which pop singer starred in the 1976 movie *The Man Who Fell To Earth*?

 27. Which metal is the best conductor of electricity?

 28. What is the national airline of Russia?

 29. Which is the largest island in the Canary Islands?

 30. Name the only palindromic record by a palindromic group.

ANSWERS: PAGE 232

31. Roger the Dodger has featured in which comic since 1953?

 32. Which king of England was born in 1885?

 33. Which of these animals can travel the fastest: a whippet, a greyhound or a coyote?

 34. What does a cryometer measure?

 35. How many dice are thrown in the casino game Craps?

 36. What colour is melanite?

 37. What famous item of clothing was designed by Mary Quant in 1965?

 38. What is the world's highest capital city?

 39. What food has a name that derives from the French for 'baked twice'?

 40. What are plants that flower every year called?

ANSWERS: PAGE 232

QUIZ 16

 1. How old was Pharaoh Tutankhamun when he died?

 2. What is 33 squared?

 3. Who had a worldwide hit with 'Mambo Number 5' in 1999?

 4. Which is the largest railway station in the world?

 5. What is the collective name for a group of crows?

 6. In which UK city are the offices of the DVLA?

 7. Which pop group's name was taken from the children's TV programme *The Banana Splits* and Roxy Music's second hit record?

 8. In a standard game, what is the highest score finish with three darts?

 9. Who played the lead role in the film *Saturday Night Fever*?

 10. What is the unit of currency in Japan?

ANSWERS: PAGE 233

11. If you sailed from Bornholm to Gotland which sea would you be in?

 12. Which football club bought Paul Gascoigne from Newcastle United in 1988?

 13. Who is fourth in line to the throne?

 14. Who is said to have betrayed Jesus for thirty pieces of silver?

 15. Who had a hit with the theme to the 1984 film *Ghostbusters*?

 16. What was the building that is now the Tate Modern used for before it was a gallery?

 17. Who is the father of Jordan's son Harvey?

 18. In which part of the human body would you find the hammer and stirrup?

 19. Which murderer did Richard Attenborough play in the film *10 Rillington Place*?

 20. Which two royal houses fought the War of the Roses?

ANSWERS: PAGE 233

21. Which is the world's longest river?

 22. In which city is the *Jerry Springer Show* filmed?

 23. Which English coin was withdrawn in 1960?

 24. Of which US state is Augusta the capital?

 25. Who was the drummer with The Jam alongside Paul Weller and Bruce Foxton?

 26. Which is the world's only flying mammal?

 27. What was the title of the 1961 Elvis film about a GI coming home to Honolulu?

 28. Which country governs the Faroe Islands?

 29. Which motor manufacturer takes its name from the Latin for 'I roll'?

 30. Who makes the teenage girls' clothes range 915?

ANSWERS: PAGE 233

31. Which goalkeeper was Wales' first choice from 1982 to 1996?

32. Who was the first female speaker of the House of Commons?

33. How many feet are there in a Roman mile: 4,600, 5,000 or 5,200?

34. Which 1980 hit for Martha & the Muffins shares its name with a 2008 TV series?

35. What is the common name for the Central Criminal Court?

36. What name was given to a piece of stretchy fabric worn by women to discos in the 1970s?

37. What is the name of the character played by John Travolta in *Pulp Fiction*?

38. What offer were we told to 'tell Sid' about in the 1986 advertising campaign?

39. What is the name of the village in Scotland where couples once eloped to marry?

40. Which Fifties star was known as the 'King of Skiffle'?

ANSWERS: PAGE 233

QUIZ 17

 1. What name is given to the tiny biscuits with blobs of icing on?

 2. Which man-made landmark took 1,700 years to build?

 3. Which wedding anniversary is traditionally celebrated with paper?

 4. What was the name of the lunar module on Apollo 11?

 5. Which knight of the Round Table is said to have found the Holy Grail?

 6. What stamps did you collect when purchasing petrol in the 1970s?

 7. Which actor played the lead role in the Nineties TV series *Spender*?

 8. Which is the most southerly country in Scandinavia?

 9. According to the rhyme, which day's child has 'far to go'?

 10. Where did pop group Toto get their name from?

ANSWERS: PAGE 233

11. On which date did it become compulsory to wear seat belts in the front of cars?

 12. What is the unit of currency in Mexico?

 13. Jacqueline Hill was the last victim of which serial killer?

 14. Who took 67 wickets in 13 matches for England in 2004?

 15. What were Starsky and Hutch's forenames?

 16. What was Adolf Hitler originally employed as?

 17. Which South American bird has the largest wingspan at up to 3 metres?

 18. Where in the body is the patella?

 19. In which country did the Tango originate?

 20. In which county is the Isle of Sheppey?

ANSWERS: PAGE 233

21. Who wrote *Frankenstein*?

 22. What was the name of the ferry that overturned outside the port of Zeebrugge in 1987?

 23. Which cosmetics company makes Shine Temptation Stars lipstick?

 24. Who said, 'There will be no white wash in the White House'?

 25. What did Prince Charles wear around his neck at the Live Aid concert?

 26. What nationality was the ex-Formula One driver Niki Lauda?

 27. Which city witnessed many deaths when a passenger jet crashed into the Potomac River?

 28. Who won an Oscar for Best Supporting Actress for the film *Tootsie*?

 29. In the phonetic alphabet, what words represent X, Y and Z?

 30. What is the state capital of Hawaii?

ANSWERS: PAGE 233

31. Where did John Lennon marry Yoko Ono in March 1969?

Let's drop these questions . . . awooga!

32. Which English queen had 17 children?

33. What is the most populated city in Europe?

34. What name is given to a thin metal strip on the neck of a guitar?

35. What points total changed from 2 to 3 in 1981?

36. Which is the longest river in Asia?

37. Which punk rocker was born William Broad in 1956?

38. In a thunderstorm why do you see the lightning before you here the thunder?

39. In which county is Bristol?

40. What does a testator make?

ANSWERS: PAGE 233

QUIZ 18

 1. When facing towards the front of a vessel is port on the left or right?

 2. What name is given to the end of a magnet?

 3. Who, in 1962, was given the biggest ticker-tape parade in history when New York showered 3,474 tons of paper on him?

 4. What is the capital of Cyprus?

 5. What was the real name of Lord Haw-Haw, who was hanged for treason in 1946?

 6. Which Ukrainian city gives its name to a chicken dish?

 7. Which comic book broke the issue record in the UK on 10 July 1999 with its 3,007th issue?

 8. What does the musical direction 'dulce' mean: sweet, soft or loud?

 9. Who was the youngest footballer to score for England in the twentieth century?

 10. Which is the world's lowest sea?

ANSWERS: PAGE 234

11. Apart from Anne Boleyn which other of his wives did Henry VIII have executed?

12. Which airport is the nearest when visiting Benidorm in Spain?

13. What white wine from Germany shares its name with a joint of ham?

14. What was the name of Britney Spears's début hit single?

15. On which river does the city of Leeds stand?

16. What is the name of Dame Edna Everage's husband?

17. In golf, what is the name of the trophy presented to the winner of the British Open?

18. In which year was Dutch artist Vincent van Gogh born?

19. Name the shorts made famous in the discos of the 1970s.

20. What is the lowest temperature recorded in England in degrees centigrade: –26.1, –21.5 or –31.6?

ANSWERS: PAGE 234

21. Who made a guest appearance in *Coronation Street* in 2004 as Shelley Unwin's love interest?

 22. Which new English coin was first introduced in 1983?

 23. Which beer shares its name with a type of fish and a rock in the Forth of Firth?

 24. Which part of London is famous for its diamond trade?

 25. Which English cricket ground staged its first test for more than 100 years in 2003?

 26. Who starred as Rosemary in the film *Shallow Hal*?

 27. What was the name of the asylum seekers' holding camp near Calais?

 28. What type of animal is Penfold, the sidekick to *Danger Mouse*?

 29. What was first broadcast from Greenwich by the BBC in February 1924?

 30. Which company, founded by Sara Blakely, is said to have revolutionized women's hosiery and underwear?

ANSWERS: PAGE 234

31. Which group of islands were the first discovered by Columbus in 1492?

 32. Which Reading-born actress won a Best Actress Oscar at the 2008 Academy Awards?

 33. Which park did the Small Faces sing about in 1967?

 34. What is the capital of the United Arab Emirates?

 35. What does a chandler make or sell?

 36. Whose hand did Dennis Healey deny kissing, saying, 'I wasn't kissing it, I was trying to bite it off'?

 37. Who will captain Europe in the 2010 Ryder Cup in Wales?

 38. How many engines has a Boeing 737 got?

 39. What is Roosevelt's Mount Rushmore portrait wearing that the other three faces are not?

 40. Which group had a hit record in the 1970s, the 1980s and the 1990s, each time with a completely different line-up?

ANSWERS: PAGE 234

QUIZ 19

 1. A car must have its first MOT after how many years?

 2. Which TV chef plays with a band called Scarlet Division?

 3. Which European country's flag is the same as the flag of Monaco but with the colours reversed?

 4. Morocco Mole was the sidekick of which cartoon character?

 5. Who was Queen Elizabeth II's first Prime Minister?

 6. How many numbers are there in a bank sort code?

 7. Who won Olympic gold for Great Britain on Valentine's Day, 1984?

 8. What is Norville's nickname in *Scooby Doo*?

 9. What was the UK's favourite toothbrush colour in 2002?

 10. Which member of Girls Aloud is from Northern Ireland?

ANSWERS: PAGE 235

11. In which sitcom did Saffron and Bubble appear?

Good luck everybody!

12. Which country has the Internet domain .za?

13. Which Chelsea footballer split from fiancée Elen Rives in 2009?

14. Who spent 27 years in exile before being allowed to address a crowd of 100,000 in Gaza?

15. Who was the first member of the British Royal Family to give birth in an NHS Hospital?

16. Which club held the FA Cup for six years?

17. Milk is rich in which vitamin?

18. Which country is the British holidaymaker's favourite destination with 12.6 million visitors in 2002?

19. Which is the world's largest inhabited castle?

20. Which triple gold-winning Olympian of 1988 died ten years later at the age of 38?

ANSWERS: PAGE 235

21. Released in 1981, which is the bestselling album in the UK?

 22. What is the national animal of South Africa?

 23. In the film *Back to the Future*, what year did Marty and Doc go back to?

 24. What is the Spanish word for 'navy'?

 25. Which imaginary line on the earth's surface lies largely at 180 degrees longitude?

 26. Which country became rugby's sixth nation?

 27. Who topped Julia Roberts and Nicole Kidman in 2003 to become the world's highest-paid actress?

 28. What is the world's biggest-selling writing implement?

 29. What is the county town of Buckinghamshire?

 30. Which movie brought stardom to Jamie Bell?

ANSWERS: PAGE 235

31. Who, in 1979, became Britain's first one-million-pound football player, breaking the British transfer record?

 32. What type of creature is an albacore?

 33. In computer terms, what is an FTP when you are online?

 34. What did Consignia become in 2002?

 35. Between 1714 and 1830 all British monarchs shared which first name?

 36. Which planet appears brightest to the naked eye?

 37. Which Australian band were one-hit wonders in 1976 with 'Howzat'?

 38. Opened in London in 1954, what was the first burger fast food restaurant in the UK?

 39. Which blonde screen legend made only eleven films, including three for Alfred Hitchcock?

 40. Which member of the British Royal Family came top in a 2003 sexiest eyes poll?

ANSWERS: PAGE 235

QUIZ 20

 1. Which Russian space station was visited by American astronauts?

 2. Which group has more teeth: mammals or reptiles?

 3. What could shops refuse to take from 12 March 1988?

 4. Which game features a top hat, a boot and a racing car?

 5. Which cult TV series featured the murder of Laura Palmer?

 6. Which country accepted the blame for the Lockerbie disaster?

 7. Which country did Mario Kempes play for?

 8. Behind the Lord Chancellor, who is the second highest judge in England and Wales?

 9. What must not be shown on television during a religious programme?

 10. Which chocolate bar was launched in 1978 by a long-distance lorry driver called Martin Fisk?

ANSWERS: PAGE 235

11. What do the individual numbers on a roulette wheel add up to?

 12. Ryan Giggs, who played international football for Wales, was born in England: true or false?

 13. Who was the lead singer of punk band The Clash?

 14. What was the name of Ernie's straight man in *Sesame Street*?

 15. What is the official residence of the Archbishop of Canterbury?

 16. Which of the six noble gases comes first alphabetically?

 17. What is the third major Balearic Island with Majorca and Minorca?

 18. What form of sentence was introduced to the UK by the 1972 Criminal Justice Act?

 19. Which is the largest county in England?

 20. What does the 'DC' in Washington DC stand for?

ANSWERS: PAGE 235

21. Who won the men's Australian Open Tennis Championship in 2009?

 22. Who provides the voice of Woody in the film *Toy Story*?

 23. Which colour can be found at the top of a rainbow?

 24. What is the maximum number of horses allowed to run in the Grand National?

 25. Which famous scientist was born in Germany in 1879, became a Swiss citizen in 1901 and later became a US citizen in 1940?

 26. Which song provided Petula Clark with her 1961 UK number one?

 27. Which three-letter word can come before 'row', 'king' or 'rage' to make three new words?

 28. Who in Greek mythology was the first woman on earth?

 29. Which Channel Four TV show's presenters included Mark Lamarr, Amanda de Cadenet and Terry Christian?

 30. According to the Bible, what kind of bird did Noah first release from the ark when the rain stopped?

ANSWERS: PAGE 235

Take your time, it's your game

31. What is the national dance of Brazil?

32. In which country would you find the world's largest pyramid by base area?

33. What is the largest landlocked country in the world?

34. Who was the first woman to win a Nobel Prize?

35. Which country is hosting the Rugby Union World Cup in 2011?

36. Which supermarket is mentioned in Chas and Dave's song 'Rabbit'?

37. What does PS stand for at the end of a letter?

38. What was the first programme to be shown on BBC2 when it launched in 1964?

39. How many times is the 'F' word used in the film *Pulp Fiction*?

40. What is the state capital of Florida?

QUIZ 21

 1. Which games console hit the shops for the first time in 1995?

 2. In 1988, which golfer became the first British winner of the US Masters?

 3. Which is the largest country in the world with a four-letter name?

 4. Who did Ted Turner, the media tycoon, marry in 1991?

 5. What is the name of the Chief Justice who gave President Barack Obama the oath incorrectly?

 6. Which children's TV show ran from 1955 to 1984?

 7. 'A word I know, six letters it contains, subtract just one and twelve is what remains.' What is the word?

 8. Cable-stayed, pontoon and suspension are all types of what?

 9. Which is the highest volcano in Europe?

 10. The theme tune to which TV show starts with the line 'Stick a pony in me pocket'?

ANSWERS: PAGE 236

11. Which city was the European 'Capital of Culture' for 2008?

 12. What did Gottlieb Daimler and Wilhelm Maybach invent in 1885?

 13. Which part of the foot is also the name of a fish?

 14. Which Barbadian singer stayed ten weeks at number one with 'Umbrella'?

 15. Who is the only driver to hold the Formula One World Championship and Indy Car Championship at the same time?

 16. How did Judith Keppel make television history in November 2000?

 17. Which animal's name means 'river horse'?

 18. Who was known as 'the lady with the lamp'?

 19. In the world of physics, what is a capital 'V' the abbreviation for?

 20. Which 'T' was the surname of the subject of the first of the *Mr Men* books?

ANSWERS: PAGE 236

21. Who was the director of the FBI from 1935 until his death in 1972?

 22. What is the name of the fictional tube station in *EastEnders*?

 23. What is the capital of Tenerife and also the name of a Blackburn Rovers footballer?

 24. Which is the only country that is landlocked with Denmark?

 25. Who replaced Dermot Murnaghan as host of the quiz show *Eggheads* in December 2008?

 26. In 1970, what did football referees get that they had not had before?

 27. Which Eighties pop star was sentenced to fifteen months in prison for assault in January 2009?

 28. The French do it on a Sunday, the Americans do it on a Tuesday, and the British do it on a Thursday. What is it?

 29. Which pop star played Adrian Mole's mother on TV?

 30. What is the normal colour of the 'black box' in a plane that can be used to gather important information in the event of a crash?

ANSWERS: PAGE 236

31. What is the name given to a female swan?

 32. Which 'P' can go before 'piece' and 'line' and after 'garden'?

 33. How many seconds delay are there between each of Big Ben's strikes: 1, 3 or 5?

 34. What is the only country that is crossed by both the equator and the tropic of Capricorn?

 35. In which county would you find Stansted Airport?

 36. Which variety of dog has breeds called Welsh, Scottish and Irish?

 37. How old is Juliet when she dies in Shakespeare's *Romeo and Juliet*?

 38. British Gas is owned by which company?

 39. Who provided the voice of the princess in the film *Shrek*?

 40. Which group provided the title music for *Friends* with 'I'll Be There For You'?

ANSWERS: PAGE 236

QUIZ 22

 1. The Radio One Roadshow was launched in 1973 by Alan Freeman at Newquay, but which DJ hosted the last ever Roadshow at Brighton in 1999?

 2. In the game *Cluedo*, which room can be accessed via the secret passageway from the study?

 3. For which drink is 'mother's ruin' a nickname?

 4. Which Euro pop group were going 'from Paris to Berlin' in 2006?

 5. Which football team is nicknamed The Rams?

 6. What is the capital of Canada?

 7. Why are there 13 stripes on the American flag?

 8. What name is given to a sound with a frequency greater than the upper limit of human hearing?

 9. Which was the first car to have a turbo-charged engine?

 10. According to the lyrics of the song by The Weather Girls, it will start raining men at just about what time?

ANSWERS: PAGE 236

11. What is the largest gland in the human body?

Welcome to the quiz of champions

 12. What colour was Coca Cola originally?

 13. The Queensberry Rules are standard rules of which sport?

 14. The Battle of Edgehill was the first battle in which conflict?

 15. In May 2006, Belfast airport officially changed its name in honour of which famous Irishman?

 16. Which Japanese toy was all the rage in 1997?

 17. Which group were 'in a melting pot' in 1969?

 18. Which actress provides the voice of Homer Simpson's mother?

 19. What name is given to an adult female hog?

 20. In which country is Interpol based?

ANSWERS: PAGE 236

21. Who is the Roman god of the sea?

 22. Which European country is the largest consumer of beer per head?

 23. In the order of the British Empire, what does the letter C stand for in CBE?

 24. What is a village without a church called?

 25. What colour are official New York taxis?

 26. What colour is the *Mr Men* character Mr Worry?

 27. *Top Gear*'s Richard Hammond features in which supermarket's TV adverts?

 28. What flavour is the liqueur cassis?

 29. Which car badges were stolen by fans of the Beastie Boys?

 30. What is the name of *The Magic Roundabout* narrator Eric Thompson's actress daughter?

ANSWERS: PAGE 236

31. In which month is Ladies' Day in the UK?

 32. Which stamp was first issued in England in 1840?

 33. What type of creature is a bonnethead?

 34. Which cosmetics company makes Full Volume lipstick?

 35. Which US rapper died on 13 September 1996 after being shot in a drive-by shooting?

 36. Bidet is the French word for what?

 37. A costard is what type of fruit?

 38. In which English county is the queen's private residence Sandringham House?

 39. Which actor was the first man to appear on the cover of American *Vogue*?

 40. What is a negatively charged electrode called?

ANSWERS: PAGE 236

QUIZ 23

 1. What is the longest river in France?

 2. What is the outermost region of a planet's atmosphere called?

 3. Which nuts are used to make marzipan?

 4. A terawatt is how many megawatts?

 5. What word describes the crime of killing a person without malice?

 6. By how many hours would you have to put your watch forward on a winter trip from London to Moscow?

 7. The first British Chamber of Commerce was founded in which city in 1783?

 8. How old was Lester Piggott when he rode his first winner?

 9. Which Eighties TV series launched the career of Robin Williams?

 10. What is the name given to a musical symbol used to indicate the pitch of written notes?

ANSWERS: PAGE 237

11. Which statesman won the 1953 Nobel Prize for Literature?

 12. What are there sixteen of in one ounce?

When I say LET'S, you say PLAY. LET'S...

 13. What was Robert I of Scotland more commonly known as?

 14. What is the capital of Colombia?

 15. Kate Moss has her own collection in which chain store?

 16. In electronics what does LED stand for?

 17. Will I Am and Fergie are members of which group?

 18. In which sport would you have used a mashie-niblick until it became obsolete in 1940?

 19. Which 1997 movie about Seventies porn films starred Bert Reynolds and Mark Wahlberg?

 20. What is a pareo?

ANSWERS: PAGE 237

21. What musical bird can fly backwards?

22. Who is the Greek goddess of victory?

23. From 1932 to 1956, Albert Pierrepoint was infamous for what?

24. What colour is the mineral amethyst?

25. What was the name of Rik Mayall's character in *The New Statesman*?

26. What delayed the 1987 Cheltenham Gold Cup for almost one and a half hours?

27. Which country has the world's largest Muslim population?

28. Under which president did the United States invade the Caribbean island of Grenada?

29. Who left Eternal in 1995 for a solo career?

30. What is the common name for the chemical ethanol: alcohol, ammonia or citric acid?

ANSWERS: PAGE 237

31. Which film hero was named after George Lucas's pet dog?

 32. Which bridge over the Thames was opened in 1831?

 33. What flows into your house at a rate of 50 cycles per second?

 34. If stone breaks scissors, what does paper do?

 35. Which northern town gave its name to the bear adopted by Children In Need?

 36. On which subject does Monty Don write and broadcast?

 37. How many stars are there on an American flag?

 38. Which two metals are mixed to produce solder?

 39. The month of January is named after which Roman god?

 40. What colour is the cabbage moth?

ANSWERS: PAGE 237

QUIZ 24

 1. In 1963, which band became the first to achieve number ones with their first three singles?

 2. What is the capital of Malta?

 3. In which English city were the MTV European Music Awards held in 2008?

 4. What word represents the letter U in the phonetic alphabet?

 5. What type of creature is a gadwall?

 6. What colour is the official Nike Premier League football?

 7. In which year was the first Miss World contest held: 1948, 1951 or 1956?

 8. Why is a jet plane always lighter at landing than at takeoff?

 9. Which fashion designer introduced the Polo label in 1967?

 10. Richard III was killed at which battle?

ANSWERS: PAGE 238

11. What was the name of Roland Rat's gerbil friend?

 12. Cambridge Favourite, Royal Sovereign and Talisman are all varieties of what?

 13. Which war was also known as the Great War?

 14. The Ivor Novello Awards honour talent in which field?

 15. Which children's TV programme, starring Richard McCourt and Dominic Wood, ran from August 2002 to March 2006?

 16. Which regiment of the Royal Navy was disbanded in 1993?

 17. What poisonous chemical element has the atomic number 33?

 18. What fish family is the anchovy a member of?

 19. In which English castle did King John die in 1216?

 20. Which strong lager reportedly increased its sales thanks to the band Bad Manners?

ANSWERS: PAGE 238

21. What is the white of an egg called?

 22. Who starred as Cyrus 'The Virus' Grissom in the 1997 film *Con Air*?

 23. Which national newspaper dropped five letters from its name in 1985?

 24. Which denomination of Scottish bank note has Balmoral Castle on it?

 25. Swansea is situated on which river?

 26. At over twelve years, which US president spent the longest time in office?

 27. Lewis Hamilton became Formula 1 World Champion in 2008, but who was the last British Formula 1 World Champion before him?

 28. What does STD stand for in the prefix on a telephone number?

 29. What type of food is quark?

 30. In which country would you find Mount Kilimanjaro?

ANSWERS: PAGE 238

31. Harry Enfield, Jon Culshaw and Alistair McGowen all provided voices for which popular TV series?

 32. What note is the top string on a six-string guitar normally tuned to?

 33. Who resigned as England cricket coach after the 2007 Ashes series defeat?

 34. Which country was at war with Iraq at the same time as Britain was at war with Argentina?

 35. Which London building was designed by G. Val Myer, built in 1932 and is presently being extended and refurbished?

 36. What was the codename of the Allied Forces landing at Normandy in 1944?

 37. Which London airport saw its first jet land in July 1988?

 38. Which actor has played James Bond the most times?

 39. What is the US state capital of Washington?

 40. What type of creature is a garibaldi?

QUIZ 25

1. What colour is the gemstone garnet?

2. Which pop band is named after an American fire truck?

3. What product was launched with Eva Herzigova and the billboard slogan 'Hello boys'?

4. What was the nuclear power station Sellafield previously known as?

5. What material is often used under a women's formal ball gown to make the skirt puff out?

6. Vancouver is in which Canadian province?

7. According to the Bible, how many of each type of animal did Moses take on the Ark?

8. In which year did decimalization take place?

9. Which animal caused the fatal wound to TV presenter Steve Irwin in September 2006?

10. What was invented in February 1991 by British scientist Tim Berners-Lee?

ANSWERS: PAGE 239

11. Which actor has starred in *Coronation Street* since the first episode in 1960?

 12. What type of animal is a Kerry Blue?

 13. What name is given to the poisonous gas emitted from a car exhaust?

 14. With what is Savile Row associated?

 15. In which tournament is the winner presented with a green jacket?

 16. Andi Peters and Emma Forbes were the original presenters of which children's TV programme?

 17. During which war was the battle of Marne?

 18. If you leave London on the M4, in which direction would you be travelling?

 19. Pussy Cat Doll Nicole Scherzinger is dating which sportsman?

 20. How many litres are in a gallon (to one decimal place)?

21. What was probed by Voyager 2 in January 1986?

It's the quiz the whole world's talking about!

22. Which Manchester band had a hit with 'This Is How It Feels'?

23. Which children's book did Richard Adams write that was made into a film in 1978?

24. What is a male horse aged five or over called?

25. What job is done by a drover?

26. Which US coin gives its name to a chocolate bar launched in 1983?

27. How many world title fights did Mohammed Ali contest under the name of Cassius Clay?

28. Who was the last British Viceroy of India?

29. What product, invented by Du Pont in 1959, revolutionized women's fashion?

30. What was *A-Team* member B. A. Baracus's worst fear?

ANSWERS: PAGE 239

31. What colour is a 500 Euro note?

It's Rob DJ on the air today

 32. In which county is Bodmin Moor?

 33. What is the gas nitrous oxide better known as?

 34. The thistle is the national symbol of which country?

 35. Who pilots Thunderbird 1?

 36. Is an alloy a pure metal or a mixture of metals?

 37. In which year was DNA discovered?

 38. Where is the Royal Navy Officer Training school?

 39. What is the fifth letter of the Greek alphabet?

 40. What is the capital of Turkey?

ANSWERS: PAGE 239

QUIZ 26

1. What is the fictional brewery in *Coronation Street*'s Rovers Return pub?

2. 'Flowers In The Rain' was the very first record played on Radio One, but who performed it?

3. What is the name given to a preparation originating in Egypt and Arabia used to darken the edges of women's eyelids?

4. Chronic hypoxia causes death due to the lack of what in the human body?

5. What does a dotted line signify on an Ordnance Survey map?

6. Who is credited as having discovered the singer Kate Bush?

7. In which country was the wheelbarrow invented?

8. Which legendary sportsman lit the flame at the Atlanta Olympic Games?

9. Who fights fires alongside Elvis Cridlington and Penny Morris?

10. From which fish is caviar obtained?

ANSWERS: PAGE 239

11. In which US city was the first Gap store opened: New York, Los Angeles or San Francisco?

 12. Introduced in New York in 1950, what was the first ever credit card?

 13. Who invented a system of shorthand in 1837?

 14. Who was elected leader of Sinn Fein in 1983?

 15. In *Oliver Twist*, what is the name of Bill Sykes' dog?

 16. What replaced the apple in the 1990s as Britain's favourite fruit?

 17. Which member of Boyzone had an autobiography entitled *Life is a Rollercoaster*?

 18. Which traveller first visited China in 1271?

 19. Which British Prime Minister had a bag named after him?

 20. Which is the largest island in the Caribbean?

ANSWERS: PAGE 239

21. Which bear celebrated his 50th birthday in October 2008?

 22. Name the colours of the five Olympic rings.

 23. In Britain, what is the only road sign to be on an inverted triangle?

 24. In which city would you find Canada's largest stock exchange?

 25. How many dots are there in total on a pair of dice?

 26. Which flag was flown by the Mayflower when the pilgrims arrived in Plymouth, Massachusetts?

 27. What would you be doing if you did a six-step, a windmill, a turtle and a hand-glide?

 28. Which company brews Harp lager?

 29. Who won the first series of *The X Factor* in 2004?

 30. Who invented the first flushable toilet in 1884?

ANSWERS: PAGE 239

31. Which motorway links Glasgow to Edinburgh?

Take your time, it's your game

32. Which is the oldest football club in London?

33. By June 2004, how many men had walked on the moon: 12, 14 or 16?

34. What are the two ingredients in a Bellini cocktail?

35. Which river flows through six European countries?

36. Which soap opera's first episode started with the discovery of the dead body of Reg Cox?

37. The company Sally Hansen specialize in which cosmetic products?

38. What was the name of David McKee's 1979 children's TV programme, a follow-up to *Mr Benn*?

39. What does a hippophobic fear?

40. In which country was actor Mel Gibson born?

ANSWERS: PAGE 239

QUIZ 27

 1. What is the one place in all of Great Britain that the queen cannot visit?

 2. What is the most common language spoken in Chile?

 3. According to the Bible, who committed the first ever murder?

 4. What is the nickname given to the Bank of England?

 5. What was the name of Mickey Mouse's dog?

 6. After Neil Armstrong and Buz Aldrin, who was the third member of the Apollo 11 mission to walk on the moon?

 7. Which UK group was banned from entering the US for unspecified reasons from 1965 to 1969?

 8. Who was the first player to play for England that wasn't yet born when England won the World Cup in 1966?

 9. What is a baby oyster called?

 10. In which country would you find Cotopaxi, the world's highest active volcano?

ANSWERS: PAGE 240

11. Who invented denim jeans?

 12. Which sea did Moses part?

 13. What was the children's favourite drink in the Famous Five books?

 14. What note do orchestras typically tune to?

 15. In computer terms you use a POP3 to receive emails via an Internet service provider, but what does POP stand for?

 16. Statler and Waldorf appeared in which children's TV series?

 17. In which year were luncheon vouchers introduced in the UK: 1952, 1954 or 1960?

 18. Arctic King, Saladin and Tom Thumb are varieties of which vegetable?

 19. How many black keys are there on a standard piano?

 20. What is the speed in knots of V1 – the point of no return in the takeoff of a jet aircraft?

ANSWERS: PAGE 240

21. Who played at both the British and American Live Aid concerts in 1985?

 22. Sir Frederick William Herschel discovered which planet on 13 March 1781?

 23. Aboard which ship did Captain Scott sail to the Antarctic in 1901?

 24. In the TV series *Andy Pandy* what was Andy's sister's name?

 25. What is the largest city on the Firth of Forth?

 26. What colour is the number 10 on the door of 10 Downing Street?

 27. Which team are the best-supported rugby team in either code?

 28. Who was ice-picked to death under orders from Stalin?

 29. What is the name of the character played by Philip Glenister in *Life on Mars*?

 30. How many different football clubs has Kevin Keegan managed?

ANSWERS: PAGE 240

31. What significant law relating to literary and artistic works was first introduced in 1709?

32. A 1983 survey claimed that nine out of ten women had what that were too small?

33. Which Swedish band had a UK number-one record with 'Cotton Eye Joe' in 1994?

34. Which former worker at the Gdansk shipyard became president of his country?

35. Which river flows through Lanark and Greenock?

36. 'CHAP JIM AND HE'S AT AGE TEN' is an anagram of which children's book and film? (4 words)

37. Which company makes the Secret Slimmer range of hosiery?

38. In *Back to the Future* what 'makes time travel possible' according to Doc?

39. Where on a horse do you find its poll?

40. How many UK monarchs were there in the 20th century?

ANSWERS: PAGE 240

QUIZ 28

 1. Where was the first Formula 1 Grand Prix at night held?

Heavy Quiz . . . after Heavy Quiz

 2. In motoring terms what does the acronym TCS stand for?

 3. Which band sacked their drummer Stuart Cable in September 2003?

 4. Which planet has the shortest year?

 5. Which British city has an underground railway system nicknamed 'The Clockwork Orange'?

 6. In which 1983 movie did Sean Connery return as James Bond?

 7. Which Olympic sport uses a planting box?

 8. Which is the biggest building society in the United Kingdom?

 9. Which former Radio 1 DJ helped 'Relax' reach number one by getting it banned by the BBC?

 10. What is the name of the bee that makes honey?

ANSWERS: PAGE 240

11. Which number is the odd one out: 37, 47, 57 or 67?

 12. In Cockney rhyming slang, what is a 'Canary Wharf'?

 13. In which US state would you find Las Vegas?

 14. Which of the following has the most calories: a medium-sized boiled egg, one teaspoon of butter or half a grapefruit?

 15. Why can't a man living in York be buried west of the Trent?

 16. Which motorway circles Manchester?

 17. After how many years of marriage is a golden wedding anniversary celebrated?

 18. Who has appeared in more Alfred Hitchcock films than anyone else?

 19. Harrisburg is the capital of which US state?

 20. Which corporation owns the brands Duracell, Braun and Gillette?

ANSWERS: PAGE 240

21. The USA won the Ryder Cup at Valhalla Golf Club in 2008, but at which golf course will the next Ryder Cup take place in 2010?

 22. Which Anglo-Swedish band released their third studio album *Slipway Fires* in 2008?

 23. Which four letters are worth 3 points each in the game of Scrabble?

 24. 'OKAY NARROW ENEMY' is an anagram of which foot-baller? (3 words)

 25. What was the name of the first purpose-built TV studios in Europe, which opened in 1968 and closed in 2009?

 26. What do Mexico City, Auckland and Naples all have in common?

 27. Which company makes the 'Cross Your Heart' bra?

 28. Who tried to emulate Phileas Fogg by going round the world in 80 days in 1988?

 29. What is the world's northernmost capital city?

 30. What animal is derived from the Latin word meaning 'sharp teeth'?

ANSWERS: PAGE 240

31. What are the names of the four American states that begin with either 'North' or 'South'?

 32. What item of clothing did Einstein claim never to wear?

 33. *The Archers* is the world's longest-running radio drama series, but which fictional village is it set in?

 34. The name of which Italian cheese means 'recooked'?

 35. What is the hard tag at the end of a shoelace called?

 36. Who was the voice of Count Duckula?

 37. Which famous film director is uncle to actor Nicolas Cage?

 38. How many points are needed to win a game of cribbage: 99, 121 or 169?

 39. From which section of the atmosphere do radio waves mainly reflect?

 40. What does FTP stand for in the world of computers and the Internet?

ANSWERS: PAGE 240

QUIZ 29

 1. In the children's TV show, what are the names of the Banana Splits?

 2. Which group, formed at a school in Oxford in the late 1980s, took their name from a song by Talking Heads?

 3. What is the collective name for a group of geese?

 4. The LHC near Geneva started the Big Bang experiment in 2008, but what does LHC stand for?

 5. Which South African cricketer was banned for life in 2000 for match fixing?

 6. What river flows through Frankfurt?

 7. How many hours behind GMT is the Pacific Time Zone?

 8. 'EXACT FORTH' is an anagram of which TV programme? (3 words)

 9. What substance is fermented to make alcohol?

 10. Which female artist had a hit with 'Love Is A Battlefield' in 1985?

ANSWERS: PAGE 241

11. What is the name of the coloured part of an eye?

 12. What are the next letters in this sequence: HW, EH, HW, JC, MT, JM, TB?

 13. In what year did the London Eye open?

 14. Benny the Ball, Choo Choo and The Brain were all characters in which cartoon series?

 15. What is the square root of 1764?

 16. At which train station is Paul Simon said to have been when he wrote 'Homeward Bound'?

 17. What animal lives in a dray?

 18. Name the only US state with a Z in its name?

 19. What element has the chemical symbol Hg?

I'm just a rascal . . . a quizzy rascal

 20. What does HMV stand for?

ANSWERS: PAGE 241

21. In *Top Gun*, what were the nicknames of the chief and his wingman played by Tom Skerritt and Michael Ironside?

 22. Who died on 5 May 1981 after 65 days on hunger strike?

 23. Who invented a method to make commercial frozen foods in 1929?

 24. Who sang the theme for the James Bond film *A View to a Kill*?

 25. In a game of poker, if you have an Ace, King, Queen, Jack and Ten of the same suit what is it called?

 26. Belarus declared independence from which country in 1991?

 27. Mr Pink and Mr Orange are characters from which Quentin Tarantino film?

 28. What do Hull City and Castleford Rugby League have in common?

 29. Which children's TV series created by Phil Redmond ran for 30 years?

 30. What were introduced to regulate motorists in 1964 and have been much revered ever since?

ANSWERS: PAGE 241

31. What is the name of the prison in Baghdad where Saddam Hussein's government carried out torture and execution?

32. Which is Britain's most northerly racecourse?

33. Which American released an album called *The Sweet Escape* in 2006?

34. What is ylang-ylang?

35. Which squeaky character became Philip Schofield's sidekick on children's TV?

36. There is a city called Rome on every continent: true or false?

37. Which is further east: Reno, Nevada or Los Angeles?

38. 'BIONIC PORTRAIT OF ARROGANCE' is an anagram of which US multinational company? (3 words)

39. Who looked in the Yellow Pages to find a shop that sold his own book about fishing?

40. Who were the last brothers to play together in a World Cup-winning team?

ANSWERS: PAGE 241

QUIZ 30

 1. Born in Selby, which English monarch ruled Britain from 1100 to 1135?

 2. Who was the original presenter of *Family Fortunes*?

 3. Which colourful singer was born Alecia Beth Moore?

 4. What appeared first on earth: spiders or dinosaurs?

 5. Which former *Big Brother* winner became a lingerie model for Ann Summers in 2006?

 6. The natives of which country share their name with a style of shoe heel?

 7. Which country has the second largest Jewish population in the world?

 8. The trumpet, tuba and cornet belong to which musical instrument family?

 9. What connects Uganda, Kenya and Ecuador?

 10. Beryl and Sandra were flat mates in which 1970s sitcom?

ANSWERS: PAGE 242

11. In which district of London would you find Harrods department store?

 12. Founded in England in the 17th century, what were the Religious Society of Friends better known as?

 13. Which Roman goddess is also a brand of margarine?

 14. Which character was convicted of arson in *Auf Wiedersehen Pet*?

 15. In 1960, the UK publishing ban was lifted on which 1928 book?

 16. In which county is Carlisle?

 17. A boomslang is what type of creature?

When I say KUNG, you say POW CHICKEN, KUNG ...

 18. Who was the first artist to appear at the new Wembley Stadium?

 19. How many natural satellites does the earth have?

 20. With which sport would you associate Nick Skelton?

ANSWERS: PAGE 242

21. What is the only word in the English language that ends in the letters 'mt'?

 22. How many valves are in the heart?

 23. 'LOCALS WANT NEW BEER' is an apt anagram of which tipple? (3 words)

 24. Who narrated children's TV programmes *Camberwick Green*, *Trumpton* and *Chigley*?

 25. Which castle was built by William the Conqueror in 1078?

 26. Which letter of the alphabet had a top-ten hit with 'Pop Musik' in 1979?

 27. Which company makes the Lipfinity lipstick range?

 28. If a football club has triangular corner flags what does this signify?

 29. What is a group of chickens called?

 30. What is Latin for 'great charter'?

ANSWERS: PAGE 242

31. What was launched by the Spice Girls on 30 March 1997?

 32. What colour is a Burmese ruby?

 33. What was the name of the backcombed hairstyle made famous in the Sixties?

 34. Tiger Woods set the US Masters tournament record in 1997, but what was his total par score?

 35. What is the tallest freestanding building in Britain?

 36. Roger Mellie 'The Man on the Telly' is a character in which comic?

 37. In measurement terms, how many links are in a chain?

 38. Who succeeded Michael Foot as Labour leader?

 39. In *The A-Team* what was 'B. A.' an abbreviation for?

 40. What is the name given to the bone in your arm commonly known as the funny bone?

ANSWERS: PAGE 242

QUIZ 31

 1. How old does a road vehicle need to be to be described as a classic?

 2. Where did serial killer Dr Harold Shipman study to become a GP?

 3. How many 'pips' are there on the Greenwich Time Signal?

 4. What is the name of Tony Manero's dance partner in the film *Saturday Night Fever*?

 5. What colour is a 100 Euro note?

 6. The Boardmasters surfing event takes place in which seaside resort every year?

 7. Which animals hate citrus smells: cats or dogs?

 8. Who scored 100 runs in his first Test Match as England captain in 2008?

 9. Which is the largest island in the Mediterranean Sea?

 10. What is the last letter in the Greek alphabet?

ANSWERS: PAGE 243

11. What was the name of the car driven by Tinker and friends Mark and Debbie?

 12. 'EACH POMMY LEGS IT' is an anagram of which event? (3 words)

 13. Who were 'turning Japanese' in 1980?

 14. What is French for duck?

 15. Where in the body is the calcaneus bone?

 16. What is the unit of currency of Venezuela?

 17. Which river runs from Settle through to Southport?

 18. At The British Soap Awards 2008, which programme won six awards?

 19. Which pop singer did Debbie Rowe marry?

 20. Still in use today, which country's flag is the oldest in the world?

ANSWERS: PAGE 243

21. Who were the last team Arsenal played at Highbury on 7 May 2006 before their move to the Emirates Stadium?

22. Who replaced Sharon Osbourne as a judge on *The X Factor* in 2008?

23. What does the Roman numeral M signify?

24. Snakes have voices: true or false?

Pens ready, papers steady, let's quiz!

25. Which leaves form the diet of the silkworm?

26. What is the capital of Libya?

27. Sand consists of silicon and what other element?

28. Who voiced the character of Mickey in the 1989 film *Look Who's Talking*?

29. What term is given to a golf course by the sea?

30. What is the colour of the dragon on the Welsh flag?

ANSWERS: PAGE 243

31. What is the first book of the Bible?

32. Which children's TV programme featured the characters George, Zippy and Bungle?

33. What is Britain's third largest airport?

34. What name is given to a cow that has not had a calf?

35. How many times has snooker player Ronnie O'Sullivan been World Champion?

36. What is the sum of the number of Commandments, the number of Sacraments of the Catholic Church, the number of deadly sins, and the number of entities in the Holy Trinity?

37. Which pop star featured in the film *Purple Rain*?

38. Which geographical location was the first word spoken on the moon?

39. 'CON BITES MALE FLESH' is an anagram of which film? (4 words)

40. The word 'henna' can be spelt using the periodic symbols of which three elements?

ANSWERS: PAGE 243

QUIZ 32

1. Which of the four main Balearic Islands is closest to Spain?

2. What was Mr and Mrs Spoon's daughter called in *Button Moon*?

3. What are Grey Dagger, Forester and Dingy Footman species of?

4. Which company make the perfume and aftershave Envy?

5. What name is given to a line on a weather map linking places of equal barometric pressure?

6. What TV programme pulled 138.5 million viewers in America in January 1996?

7. What was the name of Yuri Gagarin's spaceship?

8. Which country's national flag has the most colours?

9. What was the name of Dennis Waterman's character in the TV series *Minder*?

10. How was Belgian broadcaster Georgi Markov poisoned in London in 1978?

ANSWERS: PAGE 243

11. B&Q stores nationwide broke British law in 1989 by doing what?

 12. What is the name of the clockwork device used by musicians to keep time?

 13. In 1867, the invention of what made Alfred Nobel famous?

 14. In *Sex and the City*, Carrie and Miranda used to stop off at Magnolias to buy vanilla-flavoured what?

 15. You can sneeze in your sleep: true or false?

 16. Who wrote the TV series *Only Fools and Horses*?

 17. What did Members of Parliament receive for the first time in 1911?

 18. If you could stand on all the planets in the Solar System, which one would be the hottest?

 19. Which record company was founded by Madonna in 1992?

 20. Which actress starred as Roxy in the 2002 film version of *Chicago*?

ANSWERS: PAGE 243

21. In which country is Timbuktu?

Let's rock the quiz, general knowledge fans

 22. Which two letters appeared on the first Girl Guide hats?

 23. What is the square root of 169?

 24. Which Sixties icon joined the Pet Shop Boys on their 1987 hit 'What Have I Done To Deserve This'?

 25. What was the name of the title character of the children's TV series about a penguin?

 26. How many inches of mercury equal 1 bar (1000 millibars): 9.5, 19.5 or 29.5?

 27. In 1949, which city became the capital of West Germany?

 28. In which country would you find Durban?

 29. Which brand of soft drink is associated with the Wimbledon Championships?

30. At what type of shop did the Great Fire of London start in 1666?

ANSWERS: PAGE 243

31. Which ex-Beatle was taking a 'Photograph' in the 1973 charts?

 32. In which ocean is the island group the Maldives?

 33. How many legs does a lobster have?

 34. Who was President of the United States during the American Civil War?

 35. Which American institution closed its doors on 21 March 1963?

 36. Who painted *The Hay Wain*?

 37. Jill Morrell campaigned for the release of which hostage, who was finally granted freedom in 1991?

 38. What was the name of the cartoon series featuring the world's biggest little detective?

 39. What is the most common street name in Britain?

 40. Which British university has more students than any other?

ANSWERS: PAGE 243

QUIZ 33

1. What is the name of the only feature film starring Ant and Dec?

2. What is the only ten-letter word that can be typed using only the top row of a QWERTY keyboard or typewriter?

3. How many queens have ruled France?

4. The original Live Aid concerts were held at Wembley, London and RFK, Philadelphia on 13 July in which year?

5. If you were seated in the Bullens Road Stand, which football ground would you be in?

6. Which one of the three tenors was not Spanish?

7. Which is the lowest whole number comprised of letters in alphabetical order?

8. What is the Borsa Italiana in Milan?

9. Which album was the first to sell a million copies on compact disc?

10. Which daring raid was led by Guy Gibson?

ANSWERS: PAGE 244

11. How many James Bond movie titles are comprised of just one word?

 12. When does the Union Flag become the Union Jack?

 13. In which country was tea first grown?

 14. According to Tina Turner, what is the speed limit in Nutbush?

 15. Who was Lewis Hamilton's co-driver at McLaren Mercedes when he won the Formula One World Drivers' Championship in 2008?

 16. Which three South American countries does the equator cross?

 17. Which series was created by Jim Henson in 1983 after the success of *The Muppet Show*?

 18. How is the number one usually called in a game of bingo?

 19. What is a motorway called in Germany?

 20. In space it is impossible to cry: true or false?

ANSWERS: PAGE 244

21. In *On the Buses*, which character was played by Stephen Lewis?

 22. Who is the patron saint of Wales?

When I say pub, you say quiz ...

 23. Which Manchester band were 'the Resurrection' in 1992?

 24. In what month of the year do Americans celebrate Thanksgiving?

 25. Diane Leather became the first woman to do what in less than 5 minutes?

 26. Where was the Royal Mint until 1810?

 27. What was the name of Penry's cat in *Hong Kong Phooey*?

 28. In government, who holds the position of Chairman of Ways and Means?

 29. Which horse race would have been known as the Bunbury had it not been for the toss of a coin?

 30. Which musical is based on *Romeo and Juliet*?

ANSWERS: PAGE 244

31. If cats are feline which animals are ovine?

 32. 'I AM ENTITLED SUPER BIG' is an apt anagram of which building? (3 words)

 33. 'Weight in kilograms divided by height in metres squared' equates to what health indicator?

 34. What is the most common pub name in the UK?

 35. Who appeared on a World War I recruitment poster above the words 'Your country needs you'?

 36. What is the Spanish name for a bullfighter?

 37. Which club did Peter Crouch join in 2008 from Liverpool?

 38. What does the Internet abbreviation URL stand for?

 39. Felix Buxton and Simon Ratcliffe form which house music band?

 40. Who sang the first line of USA for Africa's 'We Are The World'?

ANSWERS: PAGE 244

QUIZ 34

 1. In which city was Terry Waite kidnapped?

 2. What is mixed with wine to make a spritzer?

 3. Who in 1986 became the world's youngest boxing heavyweight champion?

 4. Which famous sailor was born in 1758 at Burnham Thorpe in Norfolk?

 5. 'I have keys that open no locks, space but no room, and you can enter but not go inside.' What am I?

 6. Who starred as Lewis Medlock in the 1972 film *Deliverance*?

 7. Which city is on an island in the St Lawrence River?

 8. What were Opal Fruits re-branded as in 1998?

 9. In which century did the Mary Rose sink?

 10. What is the main language spoken in Chile?

ANSWERS: PAGE 244

11. In the TV show *Little Britain*, what is the name of 'the only gay in the village'?

12. How many sides does a decagon have?

13. Which Paul released his first single 'I Confess' when he was 14, and had written over 200 songs by the time he was 21?

14. What is the longest motorway in Great Britain?

15. If you were born in December and are not a Capricorn, what star sign would you be?

16. What kind of weatherproof footwear was made popular by a British duke in the 19th century?

17. In which game would you find a pung, kong and chow?

18. Name the US space station that was launched in 1973 and fell to earth in 1979?

19. In which country would you find the Port of Archangel?

20. Which English football club is nicknamed the Hatters?

ANSWERS: PAGE 244

21. What crashed in the Wall Street Crash?

 22. In Massachusetts in 1894, A.G. Spalding & Bros. invented the first official ball for which sport?

 23. 'SO FLASHY LONDONERS' is an anagram of which television programme? (4 words)

 24. Which Joe Cocker and Jennifer Warnes song featured in the film *An Officer and a Gentleman*?

 25. Designer Louis Reard popularized what piece of women's clothing in the 1940s?

 26. *Frasier* was a spin-off from which US sitcom?

 27. Who was captain of the *Titanic* on her maiden voyage?

 28. What was the first live TV satellite broadcast?

 29. Where will the British Grand Prix be held from 2010?

 30. Jimmy Choo is famous for producing what item of clothing?

ANSWERS: PAGE 244

31. In a 2003 survey, 98 per cent of people recognized Tony Blair, and 93 per cent recognized Jesus, but who was recognized by 99 per cent?

32. Who formed his first group The Gas Board in 1970 and Roxy Music in 1972?

33. Which German missed the putt that cost Europe the 1991 Ryder Cup?

34. What is the opposite of alkali?

35. Who wrote and produced the concept album *The War of the Worlds*?

36. What is the UK's biggest-selling daily broadsheet?

37. Which TV BAFTA winner gave us the catchphrase 'Gissa job'?

38. Which Derbyshire town is famous for its almond-flavoured pudding?

39. Who scored the first ever premiership hat trick?

40. Which number shares its key with the ampersand (&) on a standard keyboard?

ANSWERS: PAGE 244

QUIZ 35

1. Which spirit might bear a label with the letters XO, meaning 'extra old'?

2. Which celebrity managed to creep into Jordan's bed in *I'm A Celebrity ... Get Me Out Of Here* in 2004?

3. Prior to Spain's win at the Euro 2008 Championship, in what year was there previous win?

4. Which Irish indie-rock band had a hit with 'Big Sur' in 2003?

5. Ending in March, in which month does the coarse fishing season start in British Rivers?

6. What is the name of Hong Kong's equivalent of the Dow Jones index?

7. What shape is something that is cuneiform?

8. What type of creature is a dunnock?

9. 'MEAN OR STUFFILY' is an anagram of which game show? (2 words)

10. Which is the furthest south out of Casablanca, Houston, Tenerife and Miami?

ANSWERS: PAGE 245

11. Which 1984 Talk Talk song was covered by No Doubt in 2003?

12. Which type of biscuit shares its name with a European royal house that ruled from 1589 to 1792?

13. The headquarters of which sport are found at The Queen's Club in London?

14. What building, constructed in 1737, was designed to be the official residence of the Lord Mayor of London?

15. Which planet rotates in the opposite direction from the other planets?

16. Which king's son was known as the Black Prince?

17. The Czech Republic is associated with the manufacture of which plastic explosive?

18. In Tiddlywinks, what is the name of the piece that is flipped into the cup?

19. Which long-running comedy sitcom was filmed in Holmfirth?

20. Where was the train held up in the Great Train Robbery travelling from?

ANSWERS: PAGE 245

21. Which band were the first pop group to perform at the Louvre in Paris?

22. What name is given to the item in the House of Lords on which the Lord Chancellor sits?

23. What colour denotes a history question in the original Trivial Pursuit?

24. What were Fat Man and Little Boy codenames for?

25. If you landed at Gimpo International Airport, which country would you be in?

26. 'Be prepared' is a motto for all Scouts; what is the motto for Girl Guides?

27. Who alerted Bill and Ben to danger?

28. What brand of lager shares its name with the Latin for 'star'?

29. How much did the cheapest ticket on the *Titanic* cost: 36, 66 or 96 dollars?

30. Name the only four teams to have won the Premier League since it started in 1992.

ANSWERS: PAGE 245

31. What company started as 'Jerry and David's Guide to the World Wide Web'?

 32. Which Brit plays a sex-obsessed rock star in the film *Forgetting Sarah Marshall*?

 33. 'STROLLER ON GO, AMASSES NOTHING' is an anagram of which proverb? (6 words)

 34. What was the title of Elvis Presley's first British number one?

 35. What is hypertension more commonly known as?

 36. What high office did Boutros Boutros-Ghali hold from 1992 to 1996?

 37. What is the name of the only original member of *EastEnders* still in the programme?

 38. In which country is the city of Murcia?

 39. In Chicago, a 47-year-old woman died after falling out of bed and suffocating herself with her 52F breasts: true or false?

 40. What is the perfect score in ten-pin bowling?

ANSWERS: PAGE 245

QUIZ 36

 1. Where is the lowest point on earth?

 2. Which new English coin was first introduced in 1983?

 3. Who was the first person in Britain to own a video recorder?

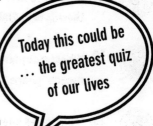
Today this could be ... the greatest quiz of our lives

 4. Name the four British racecourses that do not contain any of the letters R, A, C and E.

 5. In which city was Tony Blair born?

 6. Who plays DI Alex Drake in the TV series *Ashes to Ashes*?

 7. What is measured on the Stanford-Binet scale?

 8. By what name is singer Paul Hewson better known?

 9. Where does retired chat-show host Michael Parkinson come from?

 10. What was unique about the Apollo 17 mission in December 1972?

ANSWERS: PAGE 246

11. According to Forbes, which was the largest company in the world in 2007?

 12. What South American capital city has a name that means 'peace'?

 13. What is the name of the estate that features in the TV series *Shameless*?

 14. Which tube station on the London Underground has the most elevators?

 15. What water birds and their cries are associated with madness?

 16. If the Posh were playing the Royals at football, which two teams would be involved?

 17. Which two popular fruits are anagrams of each other?

 18. What were Regan and Carter's forenames in the *Sweeney*?

 19. What kind of party starts every two seconds somewhere in the world, generating 1.2 billion dollars a year?

 20. What is the well-known name for the Cosmonaut Training Centre in Russia?

ANSWERS: PAGE 246

21. 'LAND A CV CLAIM' is an anagram of which television presenter? (2 words)

 22. Which game did the French mathematician Blaise Pascal invent?

 23. The world's first public railway was opened in which country?

 24. Saint Isidore of Seville is the patron saint of what?

 25. The world's oldest living tree has been found in Sweden: is it 7,550 or 9,550 years old?

 26. In which year did John Major become leader of the Conservative Party?

 27. What is the title of the American equivalent to BBC's *Crimewatch*?

 28. What is the only letter that does not appear in the Periodic Table of Elements?

 29. What name is given to a baby deer?

 30. Dame Kelly Holmes was born in which English county?

ANSWERS: PAGE 246

31. Which company's jeans did Madonna promote on TV?

 32. Which river runs through New York City?

 33. By what name was the allied operation against Iraq in the Gulf War of 1991 known?

 34. Which band is fronted by Caleb Followill and includes his two brothers and cousin?

 35. An ounce of gold can be stretched into a thin wire of what length: 5, 25 or 50 miles?

 36. Scar is a wicked uncle in which animated film?

 37. What is the most commonly used word in English conversation?

 38. What quantity is measured in amperes?

 39. In which battle did Britain use radar for the first time?

 40. What is the capital of the Philippines?

ANSWERS: PAGE 246

QUIZ 37

1. In which English city is the television drama *Skins* set?

2. On which musical instrument would you find a truss rod?

3. What is the most popular paid-for UK tourist attraction?

4. Gorgonzola originates in which country?

5. What comes next in the following sequence: red, blue, white, black, orange?

6. What is Pink Floyd's only UK number-one single?

7. First published in 1937, which is the United Kingdom's longest-running children's comic?

8. 'NEXT DAY ETHICS' is an anagram of which TV series and film? (4 words)

9. The horse from the film *Toy Story 2* shares its name with which TV game show?

10. What does PVC stand for?

ANSWERS: PAGE 247

11. What does the word cenotaph mean?

 12. Which brewer was the first to introduce the 'widget' to its cans?

 13. What did Manchester United footballer Carlos Tévez put in his mouth after celebrating a goal at Christmas 2007?

 14. Which sign of the zodiac is represented by the ram?

 15. What is the first prime number greater than 50?

 16. After Asia, what is the second largest continent in the world?

 17. Who were the original presenters on Channel 4's *Big Breakfast*?

 18. What was the Spice Girls' début single called?

 19. Who was England manager after Sir Alf Ramsey?

 20. With which hobby would you associate 'twitchers'?

ANSWERS: PAGE 247

21. Where does the star appear on the flag of Cuba: on the left, right, or in the middle?

 22. Who was the Roman god of war?

 23. In 2002, who was the only musician to be voted in the top ten in the BBC's Great Britons poll?

 24. Which drink was advertised on TV by Joan Collins and Leonard Rossiter?

 25. How many days were there in February 2001?

 26. Which motor manufacturer used to make the Viva and Victor?

 27. What was the name of the Greenpeace ship that was blown up in New Zealand?

 28. Which university did Tony Blair attend?

 29. What was the most popular name given to baby girls in England and Wales in 2007?

 30. What is the F-117A Nighthawk more commonly known as?

ANSWERS: PAGE 247

31. In what year did Britain have three kings?

 32. What is the name of the fictitious town in the *Back to the Future* trilogy?

 33. In terms of land area, what was the largest empire of all time?

 34. 'OBSTINATE RATTLING' is an anagram of which TV programme? (3 words)

 35. How is Saigon now known?

 36. What was Bob Marley's backing band called?

 37. Which is the only animal that cannot jump?

 38. Who won the Golden Boot at the 1986 football World Cup?

 39. Which American state has a name that ends in three vowels?

 40. Who died on 5 May 1821, a supposed victim of arsenic poisoning from his wallpaper?

ANSWERS: PAGE 247

QUIZ 38

 1. What was the name of Han Solo's ship in *Star Wars*?

 2. If 3 cats catch 3 mice in 3 minutes, how many cats would be needed to catch 100 mice in 100 minutes?

 3. Ichthyophobia is a fear of what?

 4. Which famous artist also invented the scissors?

 5. What is the highest mountain in the Alps?

I quizzed a girl, and I liked it

 6. What type of transport appeared in London for the first time in 1861?

 7. Who is the lead singer of the Welsh band The Stereophonics?

 8. Which Apollo mission landed on the moon on 20 July 1969?

 9. What could be ballerina, broomstick or poodle?

 10. Where in the body would you be affected if you were suffering from conjunctivitis?

ANSWERS: PAGE 247

11. What's the world's most popular non-alcoholic drink?

 12. What type of musical instrument is a goombay?

 13. With five wins, which English club have won the European Cup/Champions League the most times?

 14. What is the name given to the dermatitis inflammation of the upper layer of skin called?

 15. Peter Griffin is the lead character in which animated series?

 16. In money slang, how much is a Pavarotti?

 17. What is the US state capital of Vermont?

 18. Who invented the centigrade thermometer in 1742?

 19. On a standard computer keyboard, which is the largest key?

 20. Who played Simon Gruber in the 1995 film *Die Hard: With a Vengeance*?

ANSWERS: PAGE 247

21. What is the next number in this sequence: 1, 7, 11, 5, 2?

 22. Where would you find the Ocean of Storms?

 23. The Taj Mahal is on the bank of which river?

 24. What do Americans call the boot of a car?

 25. Who won the first series of *Britain's Got Talent* in 2007?

 26. Which three countries have both a Mediterranean and Atlantic coastline?

 27. What is the most popular fruit in the world?

 28. The names of which three Scottish League football teams feature a part of the body?

 29. The 2003 film *Lost in Translation* is set in which city?

 30. Who was the last governor of Hong Kong?

ANSWERS: PAGE 247

31. How many funnels did *Titanic* have?

 32. What is France's largest vehicle manufacturer?

 33. Which girl band had a 'Cruel Summer' in 1983?

 34. What name is given to a word that is spelt the same forwards as backwards?

 35. What kind of electricity does a Van de Graaff generator create?

 36. What three flavours make up Neapolitan ice cream?

 37. Which children's TV programme launched the careers of Ant and Dec?

 38. What is the national airline of Germany?

 39. The Khyber Pass joins which two countries?

 40. In *Coronation Street*, how many sons did Mike Baldwin have?

Hit 'em with the questions babes

ANSWERS: PAGE 247

QUIZ 39

 1. Valencia Island is off the coast of which European country?

 2. 'SPOT ON EAST END' is an anagram of which Seventies sitcom? (3 words)

 3. Which cyclist has won the Tour de France the most times?

 4. On which island did the dodo live?

 5. The Savoy Grill, The Boxwood Café at The Berkeley and The Maze are all restaurants owned by which famous chef?

 6. If a male cat is called a tom, what is female cat called?

 7. What was the title of the Sex Pistol's first British hit single?

 8. What colours are the vertical stripes of the Italian flag?

 9. In which cathedral did Charles and Diana marry?

 10. Derby County set a record with only one win in the Premier League in 2008. Who did they beat?

ANSWERS: PAGE 248

11. What was the first country in the world to allow women to vote?

 12. Which motorway links the M25 to Folkestone in Kent?

 13. Who directed the 1976 film *Taxi Driver*?

 14. What does REM stand for?

 15. When did the National Lottery begin: 1993, 1994 or 1995?

 16. Which ITV programme featured on the first-class stamp to commemorate ITV's 50th anniversary?

 17. Who recorded the 1994 album *The Return of the Space Cowboy*?

 18. What is the fourth book of the Bible's Old Testament?

 19. Pearls melt in vinegar: true or false?

 20. In Monopoly, what is the cost of Old Kent Road?

ANSWERS: PAGE 248

21. Which is the oldest university in Britain?

 22. Which county was formerly called Salop?

 23. In which English city is Piccadilly rail station?

 24. The name of which English river means 'river' in Welsh?

 25. What has hands, a face and wheels?

 26. Which temperature has the same value in both Celsius and Fahrenheit?

 27. Where did Wimbledon Football Club relocate to where they were later renamed MK Dons?

 28. Which vegetable is the main source in the production of ethanol?

 29. Who founded the Tamla Motown record label?

 30. According to the proverb, all roads lead to where?

ANSWERS: PAGE 248

31. John Philip Sousa's 'The Liberty Bell' is the catchy TV theme tune to which programme?

 32. Who was known as 'The Desert Fox'?

 33. In mobile technology, what does MMS stand for?

 34. Musk, leatherback, painted and green are all examples of what?

 35. What was the name of Captain Pugwash's ship?

 36. What was the name of the plane that dropped the first atomic bomb?

 37. The British cabinet has only once held a full cabinet meeting outside London. In which Scottish city did this take place?

 38. What name is given to a cocktail consisting of tequila, cointreau and lime juice?

 39. Who returned to Yorkshire County Cricket Club as captain in 2007?

 40. Róisín Murphy is the singer in which band?

ANSWERS: PAGE 248

QUIZ 40

 1. What are the first names of the twin girls in Bart's school class in *The Simpsons*?

 2. What is the only common metal that is liquid at room temperature?

 3. What is the capital of Ghana?

> Let's rock the quiz, general knowledge fans

 4. What can be pencil, mini or micro?

 5. Which English city stands on the River Nene?

 6. What number was displayed on Damon Hill's car in both his first and second seasons for Williams-Renault?

 7. Who won the Oscar for Best Director for the 1982 film *Ghandi*?

 8. Who had their first UK number one in 1999 with 'I Want It That Way'?

 9. Which African country ranks fourth amongst the world's tea-producing nations?

10. Which was the only original ITA Franchise to survive into the 21st century?

ANSWERS: PAGE 248

11. Name the three countries in the world with the most Internet users.

12. In the children's TV series *Trumpton*, what were the names of the members of the Trumpton Fire Brigade?

13. What is the lightest WBC boxing weight?

14. What type of fictional creature was Chewbacca in the *Star Wars* films?

15. In which comedy sketch show would you find Mr Mann trying to buy things from Roy and Margaret's shop?

16. What is the largest desert in Asia?

17. What part of the body is the currency in Costa Rica?

18. Who starred as Polly Sherman in the Seventies comedy series *Fawlty Towers*?

19. In which city did the balti style of cooking originate?

20. All polar bears are left-handed: true or false?

ANSWERS: PAGE 248

21. What is the next number in this sequence: 16, 8, 11, 14, 9?

 22. Which group holds the record for the most Grammy Awards with 22 wins?

 23. In a match between Huddersfield Town and Arsenal in 1924, W. H. Smith was the first British footballer to score a goal in what manner?

 24. If you travel directly east from New York City, which country would you reach first?

 25. How many balls are on a snooker table at the start of the game, including the cue ball?

 26. In Britain, what did judges wear when passing the death sentence?

 27. Who was the first British monarch to divorce?

 28. Which is the most commonly grown fruit in the world?

 29. Which European country has the worst recycling rate?

 30. Which car manufacturer has the same name as a London bridge?

ANSWERS: PAGE 248

31. What is the name of Chesney's Great Dane in *Coronation Street*?

 32. Which George Michael song provided Robbie Williams with his first solo hit?

 33. What took the place of glass valves in a radio?

 34. How many strings does a violin have?

 35. In which American state is Fort Knox?

 36. Who is chased by Sylvester in the cartoon series?

 37. Which name is given to four strikes in a row in ten-pin bowling?

 38. Who opened the Manchester Ship Canal in 1894?

 39. Which is the only team in the 92 top English football clubs whose name starts with 5 consonants?

 40. Which footwear shares its name with the process of starting up a computer?

ANSWERS: PAGE 248

QUIZ 41

1. Which Leeds band gave us *Employment* in 2005?

2. What is one third squared?

3. What is a sea parrot more commonly known as?

You're riding with the quiz dog

4. 'WOMAN HITLER' is an apt anagram for which relation? (3 words)

5. Which type of acid is usually found in car batteries?

6. Which James Bond film features the Rio Carnival?

7. What is a mixture of fog and smoke called?

8. In 2005, Charlotte Church released an album called *Tissues and* what?

9. Which footballer made his England début in 1970 and played in 3 World Cup Final Tournaments?

10. What is the name of the powder applied to add colour to the cheeks?

ANSWERS: PAGE 249

11. In computer terms what does CAD stand for?

 12. Who lives on the Island of Sweetwater?

 13. What is the Paris underground railway system called?

 14. Which group were riding 'a white swan' in 1970?

 15. Geoffrey Howe and Nigel Lawson were two of Margaret Thatcher's three Chancellors of the Exchequer, but who was the other?

 16. Written by former MI5 operative Peter Wright, which book was banned by the British Government in 1987?

 17. Who invented the jet engine?

 18. When it ages does red wine get lighter or darker?

 19. Which sea is to the west of Denmark?

 20. Who had a hit with 'Wake Up Boo' in 1995?

ANSWERS: PAGE 249

21. In which country would you pay with a rupee?

 22. In the TV advertisement, which ice cream was stolen by a passing gondolier?

 23. How many faces does a cube have?

 24. On what platform at Kings Cross would you board the Hogwarts Express?

 25. What major war began on 10 October 1899?

 26. In the Disney film, how many of Snow White's seven dwarfs have beards?

 27. In a standard game of darts, at what height is the dartboard hung, measured from the floor to the bullseye?

 28. By what name is Schubert's Symphony No. 8 better known?

 29. Where would you find a head gasket?

 30. Which is the third closest planet to the sun in the Solar System?

ANSWERS: PAGE 249

31. In musical terms what does the abbreviation *ff* mean?

 32. Who were known on TV as the *Two Fat Ladies*?

 33. In science, what do barometers measure?

 34. What is the most northern national capital in Europe?

 35. When did women in Turkey get the vote: 1934 or 1964?

 36. What was the name of the character played by Uma Thurman in *Pulp Fiction*?

 37. Which birthday was celebrated by the Royal Air Force on 1 April 2008?

 38. What is the middle of an atom called?

 39. What is the capital of the Bahamas?

 40. What was the name of the car in *The Dukes of Hazzard*?

ANSWERS: PAGE 249

QUIZ 42

 1. Which County Cricket team fielded its first overseas player in 1992?

 2. Which country does 78 per cent of its external trade with the USA?

 3. In 1960, which country became the first in the world to have a female Prime Minister?

 4. What is the capital of Croatia?

 5. Gary, Tony, Dorothy and Deborah are all characters in which Nineties sitcom?

 6. What could be described as knee, calf or mini?

 7. During which war did Florence Nightingale become famous for her work in army hospitals?

 8. Which TV series is set on Wisteria Lane in Fairview?

 9. What is the largest flatfish species?

 10. Which voyager reached the Bahamas thinking he had reached India?

ANSWERS: PAGE 250

11. Which British Prime Minister merged the British and Irish parliaments in 1801?

 12. Brian Johnson and Angus Young are members of which Australian rock band?

 13. Who starred alongside Leonardo Dicaprio in the 1997 film *Titanic*?

 14. Who invented the ballpoint pen?

 15. Who received £24.3 million in a divorce settlement in March, 2008?

 16. Which dwarf could spin straw into gold?

 17. What does CIA stand for?

 18. In which country was Cliff Richard born?

 19. Who starred as Catwoman in the 1992 film *Batman Returns*?

 20. Who cycled from Newcastle to London in aid of Sport Relief in 2008?

ANSWERS: PAGE 250

21. In which country did the rumba originate?

 22. Which planet was the smallest in the Solar System until 2006?

 23. What colour grapes are used to make white wine?

 24. 'UNVEIL NEAR END' is an anagram of which loathed government department?

 25. Where in the human body would you find the cochlea?

 26. By what name was Colonel William Cody better known?

 27. Who presents the TV quiz show *Golden Balls*?

 28. In which decade was the CD invented: the Sixties, Seventies or Eighties?

 29. Which cult children's TV series featured cartoons of *The Three Musketeers* and *The Arabian Nights*?

 30. Who won the 2009 Rugby Six Nations Championship?

ANSWERS: PAGE 250

31. On what day of the week was the attack on the World Trade Centre?

32. What was the name of the Beatles own record label?

33. Who was the last English manager to win the Premier League?

34. Who would use a gavel?

When I say QUIZ , you say TIME , QUIZ …

35. What colour is paprika?

36. How many zeros are in a million when written in digits?

37. What is the name of Del and Rodney Trotter's local in *Only Fools and Horses*?

38. Which US state has the longest shoreline?

39. What is Jennifer Beale's day job in the 1983 film *Flashdance*?

40. What is the other name given to a castle in chess?

ANSWERS: PAGE 250

QUIZ 43

 1. Which Nineties boy band kicked off their 2006 reunion tour in Newcastle?

 2. Who was the first cricketer in history to take 300 test match wickets?

 3. In which town are the administrative headquarters of North Yorkshire?

 4. Which politician was nicknamed Tricky Dicky?

 5. Who assassinated John Lennon?

 6. In children's TV, whose archrival was Dr Claw?

 7. What is the main ingredient of a soufflé?

 8. Who scored for England against France in 27 seconds of the 1982 World Cup finals?

 9. Which country was ruled by the Shoguns from 1192?

 10. Which branch of mathematics is concerned with lengths, areas and volumes?

ANSWERS: PAGE 251

11. Which port is known as the 'Gateway to India'?

 12. 'KEN GIRLY EAR' is an anagram of which TV presenter?

 13. What is a microchip usually made from?

 14. What was Marilyn Monroe's character's nickname in the film *Some Like it Hot*?

 15. Who retired from boxing in February 2009 with an undefeated record?

 16. Which musician's only UK Solo number one was 'If I Was'?

 17. What word links a train station to a type of shoe?

 18. Which zodiac sign has the symbol of the bull?

 19. Why was Carole Hersee seen on television every day from 1967 to 1997?

 20. What type of food is Bombay Duck?

ANSWERS: PAGE 251

21. In the game of roulette, what is a bet on numbers 1–18 called?

 22. In which European country is the port of Bergen?

 23. Where would you wear a slip?

Put those pens where I can see them

 24. Which Commonwealth country celebrated its bicentennial in 1988?

 25. What was odd about the Stepford wives?

 26. Which film included the song 'Wandering Star'?

 27. In sailing, what is an MOB?

 28. What was crossed on foot for the first time in 1968–69?

 29. Which two letters are the chemical symbol for copper?

 30. Where was the epicentre of the UK earthquake that measured 5.2 on the Richter Scale in 2008?

ANSWERS: PAGE 251

31. Which Irish indie band sang about 'Santa Cruz' in 2003?

 32. Who lived at 29 Acacia Road, Nuttytown?

 33. How many lanes are there in an Olympic-sized swimming pool?

 34. What is a young penguin called?

 35. Which pop diva went on the Showgirl tour in 2005?

 36. Where is the Ceremony of The Keys held every evening?

 37. Which South American city has the famous Copacabana beach?

 38. Who was Britain's highest-ranked tennis player in 2009?

 39. Who presented *Live and Kicking* with Zoë Ball?

 40. On a keyboard, the letters F to L are in alphabetical order from left to right, but which letter is absent from the sequence?

ANSWERS: PAGE 251

QUIZ 44

 1. What is the highest amount of money that can be won on the programme *Deal or No Deal*?

 2. How many minutes long is a round in boxing?

 3. What represents a battle site on an Ordnance Survey map?

 4. Was Saint Winifred the patron saint of painters or bakers?

 5. On which river was Rome built?

 6. Which Roman god was the month of March named after?

 7. Which TV show in America made a star out of Kelly Clarkson?

 8. How is the letter 'O' represented in Morse Code?

 9. By what name is a Cub Scout pack leader known?

 10. In yachting, what are sheets?

ANSWERS: PAGE 251

11. Which actor was the longest serving *Doctor Who*?

 12. What are the names of the two universities in Leeds?

 13. Which royal served a tour of duty in Afghanistan in 2008?

 14. In which country are cows considered sacred?

 15. What pace falls between a horse's trot and a full gallop?

 16. Which billionaire businessman began his career by selling plastic ducks from a small apartment?

 17. Who had a hit in 2005 with 'The Avenue', which sampled The Maisonettes' Eighties hit 'Heartache Avenue'?

 18. What river are the Victoria Falls on?

 19. What number does Johnny Wilkinson wear when playing rugby for England?

 20. What is housed in the Jodrell Bank?

ANSWERS: PAGE 251

21. What was the name of the Jewish girl whose published diary relates her time in hiding from the Nazis?

 22. In the Chinese calendar, what is 2008 the year of?

 23. 'TRUTH NOT TOP SHAME' is an anagram of which football club? (2 words)

 24. Which Australian was the victim of a tragic accident on the Great Barrier Reef in 2006?

 25. Which designer shoes have a trademark red leather sole?

 26. Mark King was the lead singer with which Eighties band?

 27. Who holds the all-time goal-scoring record in the Scottish Premier League with 173 goals?

 28. Which soap moved from BBC One to Channel Five in 2008?

 29. What is special about 4 May 2006 at two minutes and three seconds after one o'clock in the morning?

 30. Sofia is the capital of which country?

ANSWERS: PAGE 251

31. Who owned the first wristwatch: Queen Elizabeth 1 or King Louis XII?

 32. On which daytime show would you find Coleen, Kaye, Carol and Jane?

 33. In which city would you find the Avenue of the Americas?

 34. Who declared Britain a republic in 1649?

It's all to play for, and this time it's going to be fierce

 35. Which of Heather Mills' legs is artificial?

 36. Which crop is attacked by the Colorado beetle?

 37. What was the name of Oasis' 1994 début album?

 38. What are the four main blood groups?

 39. The flag of Denmark is composed of which two colours?

 40. What was Margaret Thatcher's maiden name?

ANSWERS: PAGE 251

QUIZ 45

1. What was the bear called in children's TV programme *Rainbow*?

2. From where did the *Titanic* set out on its maiden voyage?

3. In the IC codes used by British police to describe the ethnicity of a suspect. What does IC1 represent?

4. Which Russian did Boney M sing about in 1978?

5. Who narrated the *Mr Men* series on TV?

6. Which football player has cost the most money in accumulated transfer fees during his career?

7. Which word could go before star, tea and dress to make three two-word phrases?

8. In Australia, what is the alternative name for Uluru?

9. What was the name of the comet that was visible from Earth in 1997?

10. 'ONLY I CAN THRILL' is an anagram of which US politician? (2 words)

ANSWERS: PAGE 252

11. Amy Winehouse, Steve Winwood and The Zutons have all had hits with which girls' name?

12. How many pints are there in 1 litre?

13. 0131 is the dialing code for which British city?

14. For what reason was Royal Mail in the news in 1937, Oxo in 1959 and Ben Nevis in 1980?

15. What is the name of the cement mixer in the children's TV series *Bob the Builder*?

16. Which sitcom family drinks in *The Feathers*?

17. Which artist is the most successful BRIT Award winner with 15 awards?

18. On the London Underground, which is the busiest station on the Bakerloo Line?

19. Which darts player was nicknamed 'The Crafty Cockney'?

20. In which film would you find Mr Potato Head?

ANSWERS: PAGE 252

21. Which is the most populous capital city in Africa?

22. Duffle coats are named after a town in which country?

23. Whose 1992 album *Gold* has sold 25 million copies worldwide?

24. In 1979, which English art historian was exposed as a former Soviet spy and stripped of his knighthood?

25. The insecure female character whose catchphrase was 'Does my bum look big in this?' featured in which Nineties comedy show?

26. In which year did ITV commence broadcasting?

27. If you are suffering from scurvy, what vitamin are you deficient in?

28. What was the name of the 1993 film about the early years of The Beatles?

29. At which test match ground did Geoff Boycott score his 100th first class century?

30. What is the total number of eyes visible on the Jacks in a standard pack of playing cards?

ANSWERS: PAGE 252

31. Which bridge had the longest span when it opened in 1932, and is now the fourth longest?

32. What creature has the longest lifespan?

33. Which form of timepiece has the most moving parts?

34. Which New Zealand-born singer had his debut hit with 'Gotta Get Thru This' in 2001?

35. What was the name of Russ Abbot's bungling super hero?

36. London's Monument was built to commemorate which historic event?

37. Other than David Bowie, which two pop stars appear in the video for 'Ashes to Ashes'?

38. 'I SOONER ACT ROTTEN' is an anagram of which TV programme? (2 words)

39. What is the chemical symbol for silver: Gu, Ag or Si?

40. Which British fashion designer and high street store owner died in 1985, aged 60, after falling down the stairs?

ANSWERS: PAGE 252

QUIZ 46

1. In which country was Henry II of England born?

2. What is 85 per cent of 1,660?

It's quiz time, two thousand and nine, with me, Rob DJ

3. Which is the only English football club beginning with the letter Q?

4. Covering half the surface of the world, which is the largest ocean?

5. In tennis, in which country is the first Grand Slam tournament of the year held?

6. What was the name of Roger Rabbit's wife?

7. Which city in Algeria shares its name with a cosmetic product?

8. Name the four instruments in the brass section of an orchestra?

9. What is the capital of Latvia?

10. Which former leader of the PLO died in November 2004?

ANSWERS: PAGE 252

11. According to the rhyme, one is for sorrow but what is five for?

 12. What name was given to the red beret-wearing New York vigilantes?

 13. Which German invented the first one-and-a-half horsepower car?

 14. Which organ is damaged by an overdose of Paracetamol?

 15. In *An Officer and a Gentleman*, what is the name of Richard Gere's character?

 16. In which city was the Yorkshire Ripper finally caught?

 17. In which part of the human body are the metatarsals?

 18. What colour is the rose of York?

 19. How many miles per hour must the DeLorean in *Back to the Future* reach before it can travel through time?

 20. Who was England manager in the 1998 World Cup Finals?

ANSWERS: PAGE 252

21. Which naval base in Hawaii is home to the United States Pacific Fleet?

 22. Which famous encyclopedic website was founded by Jimmy Wales in 2001?

 23. What is another name for a tumblebug?

 24. 'BILGE! BBC TERRITORY, EH' is an anagram of which reality television show? (3 words)

 25. Which river separates Manchester from Salford?

 26. Which actress from *Sex and the City* was born in Widnes in 1956?

 27. In golf, how many shots is a condor or vulture?

 28. What name is shared by a small dagger and a woman's shoe?

 29. Which musical instrument family does the bassoon belong to?

 30. Who was the last ever president of the USSR?

ANSWERS: PAGE 252

31. Lincoln is the capital of which US state?

 32. Which actress starred as Princess Leia in the *Star Wars* trilogy?

 33. How old was Stanley Matthews when he made his England debut: 17, 19 or 20?

 34. Which American rock band is fronted by Michael 'Flea' Balzary?

 35. Which sea is to the west of Denmark?

 36. Which sign of the zodiac is symbolized by a water bearer?

 37. Which common metal is represented by the letters Sn?

 38. The M11 connects London with which other city?

 39. Who co-presents *Dancing on Ice* with Phillip Schofield?

 40. In Saudi Arabia, a man who was caught with two chocolate liqueurs in an airport was sentenced to 75 lashes: true or false?

ANSWERS: PAGE 252

QUIZ 47

 1. Which two world leaders are impersonated in the video for Frankie Goes to Hollywood's number one 'Two Tribes'?

 2. Which animal does not have vocal chords: the kangaroo or the giraffe?

 3. Which member of the Royal Family was married in 1960?

 4. What is the name of Jack's cat in the film *Meet the Parents*?

 5. Which British Prime Minister declared war on Germany in 1939?

 6. Who was the youngest President of the USA?

 7. Who scored the winning goal in the Chelsea victory over Manchester United in the 2007 FA Cup Final?

 8. What was introduced in 1974 to conserve electricity?

 9. In which musical does the song 'You'll Never Walk Alone' feature?

 10. Which river flows through Nottingham?

ANSWERS: PAGE 253

11. Which song won the 1995 Britpop battle between Oasis and Blur?

 12. What are Dr Peter Venkman, Dr Raymond Stantz and Dr Egon Spengler collectively known as?

 13. Who is Nigella Lawson's famous ex-politician father?

 14. 'BRINGING DREAM' is an anagram of which Oscar winning actress? (2 words)

 15. What type of animal is a squitten?

 16. Which is the only fish able to hold objects in its tail?

 17. What was Michael Jackson advertising when he was nearly killed?

 18. What is the only US state that borders only one other?

 19. Which TV series clocked up 236 episodes from 1994 to 2004?

 20. Who released her début album *Can't Take Me Home* in 2000?

ANSWERS: PAGE 253

21. Who was King of England at the time of the War of Independence?

 22. Which horse won the 2009 Grand National despite odds of 100:1?

 23. Which comic first appeared on the 4 December 1937?

 24. Who is the only golfer to have won and lost the Open Championship on a play off?

 25. In which European city are the headquarters for Interpol?

 26. What is the hardest natural substance?

 27. During what century was Napoleon Bonaparte the Emperor of France?

 28. Who allegedly sang about Warren Beatty in the 1972 song 'You're So Vain'?

 29. The anniversary of how many years of marriage is represented by silk?

 30. How old do you have to be to legally buy a lottery ticket in the UK?

ANSWERS: PAGE 253

31. What type of Fifties women's skirt shares its name with a breed of dog?

 32. Which letter is most frequently used in the English language: C, P or Y?

 33. In the cartoon series *Wacky Races*, who drove the Compact Pussycat?

 34. What river forms a large part of the boundary between Mexico and the USA?

 35. What type of nut is used to make pesto?

 36. Which sport would you be watching if you were at Happy Valley in Hong Kong?

 37. Which group sang the song used as the theme tune to *The Royle Family*?

 38. What was the name of Dido's 2003 album that featured 'White Flag'?

 39. What is a young elephant called?

 40. How many squares are there on a scrabble board?

ANSWERS: PAGE 253

QUIZ 48

 1. In Morse Code, which letter is represented by a single dot?

 2. Who is Kate Hudson's famous actress mother?

 3. Which model of Boeing Jet was involved in the British Airways Heathrow crash-landing in 2008?

 4. What sugar is found in milk?

 5. What is the largest city in Switzerland?

 6. In *Only Fools and Horses*, by what name did Trigger always call Rodney?

 7. What colour is a custard-apple?

 8. What is the highest rank in the Royal Navy?

 9. Who portrayed Brian Clough in the 2009 film *The Damned United*?

 10. What number does the letter 'D' represent in Roman numerals?

ANSWERS: PAGE 254

11. What cosmetic product was invented by Eugene Rimmel in the 1830s?

 12. In which country did Karl Marx spend the last 34 years of his life?

 13. Which Eighties duo won the Outstanding Contribution to Music award at the 2009 BRIT Awards?

 14. Which Seventies bike had a gearshift on its crossbars?

 15. How many prongs are on the crown of the Statue of Liberty?

 16. Which famous comedian used the name Gerald Wiley when he submitted scripts to the BBC?

 17. Who was the Greek god of love?

 18. How is the number eight usually called in a game of Bingo?

 19. In a game of chess, which piece is worth more: a rook or a knight?

 20. What is the state capital of Florida?

ANSWERS: PAGE 254

21. What word can precede band, tree and stamp to form three new phrases?

 22. The Clarence Hotel in Dublin is owned by two of the members of which band?

 23. Which team did Fernando Alonso rejoin for the 2008 Formula One season?

 24. How many stars are on the European Union flag?

 25. 'CORNY MALE JERKS' is an anagram of which TV presenter? (2 words)

 26. Where did Charles Darwin succeed Charles Dickens?

 27. Which artist released an album and movie under the same title of *Get Rich or Die Tryin'*?

 28. What was the name of the cabin boy in *Captain Pugwash*?

 29. Which country sends the most international post?

 30. Prior to Barack Obama, who was the last democrat President of the United States?

ANSWERS: PAGE 254

31. In computer networking, what does LAN stand for?

 32. Of all the rooms in a game of Cluedo, which would come first alphabetically?

 33. In what year did Steve Redgrave win his first Olympic gold medal?

 34. What is the highest achievable break in snooker?

 35. What was the operational squadron number of the Dambusters?

 36. What type of food is a rollmop?

 37. Who, upon splitting with her partner, said, 'At least I can wear high heels now'?

 38. How many loaves and fishes did Jesus use to feed the 5,000?

 39. What vegetable is the national emblem of Wales?

 40. Who were in the 'Church of the Poison Mind' in 1983?

ANSWERS: PAGE 254

QUIZ 49

 1. How many tiles are used in the game mahjong: 100, 121 or 144?

 2. Who directed the 2005 film *Pride and Prejudice*?

 3. What type of animal is a cachalot?

 4. What was the new name for the Millennium Dome when it re-opened in 2007?

 5. Why was teacher Gillian Gibbons in the news in 2007?

 6. On what date was the smoking ban introduced in England?

 7. Which country won the 2007 Cricket World Cup?

 8. In January 2007, which single became only the second ever to top the charts on downloads alone?

 9. Which former leader of Russia died in April 2007?

 10. Which river burst its banks in June 2007 causing severe flooding in Toll Bar, near Doncaster?

ANSWERS: PAGE 255

11. How many teaspoons make one tablespoon?

12. Who got a new post as international envoy in the Middle East in June 2007?

13. What is the name of the seventh and final Harry Potter book, released on 21 July 2007?

14. Who had hits in the Seventies with 'Everybody Dance' and 'Good Times'?

15. Which country will host the 2014 Football World Cup?

16. Which ex-Radio 1 DJ died of a heart attack in his sleep in December 2007?

17. Which author was knighted in June 2007, angering the Muslim population?

18. What was Paris Hilton's offence for which she was sentenced to 45 days in prison?

19. What country celebrated its 60th anniversary of independence from British rule on 15 August 2007?

20. Which group, named after a US state, had a hit with 'Black Eyed Boy'?

ANSWERS: PAGE 255

21. Who was appointed England football manager in December 2007?

 22. Which UK high street women's fashion store opened their first shop in New York in 2009?

 23. What Cumbrian town was used as the pilot for the digital TV switchover?

 24. In which year did Royal Mail introduce self adhesive stamps: 2001, 2003 or 2005?

 25. Which English word would be pronounced the same even if you took away the last four letters?

 26. In the TV series *Lost*, what was the oceanic flight number that crashed?

 27. If a golfer loses a ball, what is the penalty?

 28. From what type of stone is the Taj Mahal built?

 29. Who had a 1998 hit with a song named after the two main characters in *The X Files*?

 30. How many points were scored for each dot swallowed by Pacman?

ANSWERS: PAGE 255

31. 'LAZE ACHE JOG' is an anagram of which boxer? (2 words)

 32. How far would a London bus travel on a full tank of petrol if driving around the city at an average of 30 miles per hour?

 33. Who founded The Body Shop?

 34. Who overtook Bobby Moore's record of 108 England caps in March 2009?

 35. What is the name of the villain in the Bond film *Diamonds Are Forever*?

 36. What does HP stand for on a bottle of sauce?

Let's get down to quizziness

 37. Which American state is known as the Lone Star State?

 38. In which four countries might you find a Disneyland?

 39. Where was The Who's live album recorded in 1970?

 40. What numeric term describes perfect eyesight and a form of cricket?

ANSWERS: PAGE 255

QUIZ 50

 1. The River Wensum runs through which English city?

 2. In a deck of cards, what is the total value of only the numeric cards in all suits?

 3. What was the name of the Sunday-afternoon game show hosted by Jim Bowen?

 4. Which actor sang 'I Could Be So Good For You', the theme tune to *Minder*?

 5. What is the name of the volcano in Washington that erupted in 1980?

 6. In what country was Fidel Castro born?

 7. Which convenience store had a hit with 'Brimful of Asha' in 1998?

 8. The anniversary of how many years of marriage is represented by wood ?

 9. Which is the USA's only state capital that includes the name of the state?

 10. Which is the oldest of the Royal Parks in London?

ANSWERS: PAGE 255

11. What are the values of A, B and C if A+B+C = 40; A+A+B = 33 and C+C+C = 60?

 12. Which jockey won the Prix de l'Arc de Triomphe and the following day was on trial at the Old Bailey?

 13. How many satellites does Uranus have?

 14. What was the name of Alexander the Great's horse?

 15. What famous building did John Nash rebuild in 1825?

 16. What was discovered in Abraham Lincoln's coffin when it was opened in 1901?

 17. What do paleontologists study?

 18. In which city is the film *Trainspotting* set?

 19. On a standard clothing label, what does a scored out black triangle represent?

 20. Which is the biggest airline in the world by fleet size?

ANSWERS: PAGE 255

21. Which team appeared in the last and first FA Cup finals held at the old and new Wembley Stadiums?

 22. Which soul singer was dancing the 'Land of a 1,000 Dances' in 1962?

 23. What type of French missile sank two British ships in the Falklands War?

 24. Which breakfast cereal celebrated its centenary in 1994?

 25. What do the initials HB on a pencil stand for?

 26. Who manufactured the games console that featured Sonic the Hedgehog and Alex Kidd?

 27. Who invented the safety elevator in 1852?

 28. In computing, what does HDD stand for?

 29. What was Fred Flintstone's neighbour and friend called?

 30. In the Bible, to whom did god give the Ten Commandments?

ANSWERS: PAGE 255

31. What was the surname of the French brothers who established a tyre company in 1888?

32. Which comedian's characters included Marcel Wave and Cupid Stunt?

33. If you travel one mile south, one mile east and one mile north and finish back where you started from, where on earth are you?

34. How many balls are used in a game of pool?

35. Which album released on 30 November 1982 has sold over 100 million copies worldwide?

36. Which fashion house makes J'adore perfume?

37. What is the capital of Israel?

38. Who beat Ricky Hatton in the tenth round in Las Vegas in December 2007?

39. Name the word in which the first 2 letters indicate a male, the first 3 letters indicate a female, the first 4 letters indicate a great man and the whole word is a great woman?

40. What was the last year in which the home nations did not have a team in the Euro Championships Finals: 1980, 1984 or 1988?

ANSWERS: PAGE 255

Answers

What's the answer Rob?
What's the answer Rob?
That's what they say to me,
Cos this is my job,
But y'all have to wait,
To find out your fate,
I got all of your scores,
After this re-cord.

Quiz 1

1. The President of the USA
2. Melbourne
3. Central Line
4. Winston
5. Aardvark
6. Roger Sanchez
7. 9pm in winter or 8pm in summer, since Japan does not have Daylight Saving
8. Brad Pitt
9. C and B
10. Orchestral Manoeuvres in the Dark
11. Australia
12. 126
13. *Mr Benn*
14. India
15. Manchester Ship Canal
16. Darius Danesh
17. Iraq
18. George Harrison
19. Liverpool and Aston Villa
20. *The Beach*
21. 'Way Down'
22. 1946
23. KLM
24. Jack Frost
25. Frank Bruno
26. Statue of Liberty
27. Cliff Bennett and the Rebel Rousers
28. 15
29. Chris Woods
30. Jean Paul Gautier
31. Pan Am Lockerbie bombing
32. Keith Lemon (Leigh Francis)
33. Barry White
34. London
35. 24
36. The same dress size
37. They were both born on Christmas Day
38. Russell Watson
39. Durham
40. Suggs

Quiz 2

1. Between 13 and 18 million
2. Yugoslavia
3. One Canada Square, Canary Wharf
4. Frederick Forsyth
5. Leeds United
6. Python Lee Jackson
7. Pb
8. Lake Garda
9. Stockholm
10. Rachel Green
11. John Major
12. Los Angeles
13. Durham
14. Rachel Stevens
15. The Birds' Nest
16. Cuban Peso
17. Steve Strange
18. Nottingham
19. In the foot
20. Follicle
21. *Abbey Road*
22. Everton
23. *Wisden Cricketers' Almanack*
24. Waterloo
25. MCMXCVIII
26. Bill Shankley
27. M C Hammer
28. Calcutta
29. Sulphuric acid
30. River Plym
31. *For Your Eyes Only*
32. Tower 42, formerly The NatWest Tower
33. *The Seven Year Itch*
34. Clout
35. Mohammed Ali and George Foreman
36. Joan of Arc
37. Michael Schumacher
38. John Howard
39. Albatross
40. Dustin Hoffman

Quiz 3

1. Sir John Houblon
   (first Governor of the Bank of England)
2. Gnasher
3. Paul Gascoigne
4. The McCoys
5. Sacramento
6. Calvin Klein
7. *West Side Story*
8. Greyhound
9. A prial of threes
10. Corsica
11. Max Factor
12. Charles and Eddie
13. Pub opening hours
14. Alex Parks
15. Denis Compton
16. Po River
17. Cocaine
18. Donna Karan New York
19. 604,800 seconds
20. Sri Lanka
21. *Steptoe & Son*
22. Russia
23. Pencil skirt
24. Q and Z
25. Thomas Edison
26. Desert Orchid
27. Threadneedle Street
28. Joseph Stalin
29. Malibu
30. Michael Caine
31. Putter
32. 1940
33. The Four Seasons
34. Willy Wonka
35. Alexander Fleming
36. Joey
37. Wales
38. Holme Moss, Huddersfield
39. Manila
40. The Saturdays

Quiz 4

1. Table Mountain
2. A hooped underskirt
3. George Harrison
4. Dog License
5. £500
6. Hungerford
7. Edith Bowman
8. The modern bra
9. Torquay
10. Nepal
11. Odyssey
12. Austria
13. *The Italian Job*
14. Kenzo
15. £1,000
16. SCUBA
17. Anne Boleyn
18. Mumbai
19. Gandhi
20. Robbie Williams
21. Lego
22. Sea battle
23. Afghanistan and Azerbaijan
24. James Dyson
25. Cheetah
26. 'Wuthering Heights'
27. Lennon's
28. Helsinki
29. Peroxide
30. Pulp
31. Alex Ferguson
32. Bill Gates
33. Amsterdam
34. Brown
35. Sarah Michelle Geller
36. 14
37. 156
38. The storming of the Bastille
39. Professor Yaffle
40. Russia

Quiz 5

1. The Ting Tings
2. Joe Louis
3. Dallas, Texas
4. Italy
5. Lois Lane
6. Poison
7. Juneau
8. Connie Francis
9. 452
10. Margaret Beckett
11. Digital Versatile Disc
12. Nylon
13. *The Deep*
14. Ted Heath and Harold Wilson
15. A whale
16. U-2
17. Right-handed
18. Full of woe
19. Hartsfield-Jackson Atlanta International Airport
20. 19
21. Edinburgh Castle
22. *Dirty Dancing*
23. Chemical Ali
24. Suffolk
25. Lincoln City
26. Norman Cook
27. Adam Crozier
28. 3 hours
29. 5
30. Bill Wyman
31. Aristotle Onassis
32. Bustier
33. São Paolo, Brazil
34. Alexandra Palace
35. Max Headroom
36. Fred and Rose West
37. Dean Martin
38. Tin
39. Leatherslade Farm
40. A flower

As always, my answers are final

Quiz 6

1. Isambard Kingdom Brunel
2. Fifties (1959)
3. Thomas Harris
4. *Pet Sounds*
5. Glasgow Celtic
6. Peter Sellers
7. Love Kylie
8. CBGB
9. Queen Anne
10. Perth
11. Marty McFly
12. A coffin made of terracotta
13. Xylophone
14. A tree
15. 29 days 13 hours
16. Air Lingus
17. Key Largo
18. Coq au vin
19. Lily Savage
20. 1,625
21. Bad Manners
22. Today is Saturday watch and smile
23. Altitude
24. Swiss
25. He gatecrashed Prince William's
    21st birthday party
26. Brooklyn and Bronx
27. Sarah Louise Platt
28. Wellington
29. A bird
30. Acetone
31. Hamstrings
32. 4,000
33. Anthony Newley
34. Screwdriver
35. Skegness
36. Andrei Kanchelskis
37. Primary colours
38. Chicago and Los Angeles
39. Steve Harley
40. Making horseshoes

Quiz 7

1. Tiberius
2. Victoria
3. Micro skirt
4. Vincent van Gogh
5. George W. Bush
6. *Orca*
7. York
8. 1845
9. Joseph Stalin
10. Jason Robinson
11. Beyoncé Knowles
12. Wiltshire
13. Gary Jules
14. 8
15. Sneezy
16. Caustic soda
17. Cindy Crawford
18. France
19. The Kwik-E-Mart
20. The torpedo
21. 7
22. Noel Edmonds
23. The Boomtown Rats
24. Clarice Starling
25. Arizona
26. Fashion Rocks
27. Rome
28. Sir Robert Walpole
29. *Beautiful World*
30. Liverpool and Hull
31. Ben Elton
32. Angel Falls
33. Buzz Aldrin
34. The Severn
35. Yellow
36. Gatwick
37. 240
38. They both have moles above their lips
39. The Pet Shop Boys
40. English

Quiz 8

1. Dynamo
2. Meccano
3. 32
4. Strawberry
5. Colon
6. A
7. Axel Foley
8. 12
9. York
10. Tom, Dick and Harry
11. A river
12. Boogie Pimps
13. *Slumdog Millionaire*
14. Prunes
15. Memphis, Tennessee
16. Strangeways, Manchester
17. A vegan
18. Red, blue, white, yellow, green and orange
19. Loch Lomond
20. Belgium
21. Lionel Ritchie
22. PC Plod
23. Panther
24. Sugarloaf Mountain (Pão de Açúcar)
25. 33 (it is not a prime number)
26. Red
27. Sudan
28. The Epsom Derby
29. Brownies
30. Bolivia
31. Janet Ellis
32. Gerald Ford
33. Henry VIII
34. 15
35. *Cutty Sark*
36. Sigourney Weaver
37. Madonna
38. 180 degrees
39. Ho Chi Minh
40. Badminton

Quiz 9

1. Knebworth
2. Spain
3. A puma
4. Penrod Pooch
5. James Brown
6. Belarus
7. Paul McCartney
8. Toyota Corolla
9. Barbados
10. Vitamin A
11. The Queen's Speech
12. White
13. Northern Line
14. The Lev
15. Doris Day
16. 'A Day In The Life'
17. False eyelashes
18. The Black Panther
19. Payne Stewart
20. Superior
21. Soft Cell
22. Heath Ledger
23. A colony, a rookery or a waddle
24. Liverpool
25. Shoes
26. Islamabad
27. The Live Aid Concert
28. The Liffey
29. Boomtown Rats
30. Typhoid
31. Doc
32. Orange
33. Rose
34. Riviera
35. Calcutta
36. Christian Dior
37. Sheffield
38. The Foundations
39. Rutland
40. Friday 1 September 1939, with the invasion of Poland

Quiz 10

1. Concorde
2. Polar bear
3. Danger Mouse
4. Overhead Cam
5. David Bowie
6. Maybelline
7. Andes
8. Abbey Road
9. James Dean
10. Birmingham
11. 1997
12. 1971
13. Canada
14. 12
15. Phil Taylor
16. Steffi Graf
17. *Bugs Bunny*
18. Yves Saint Laurent
19. Oasis
20. The Royal Engineers
21. The River Taff
22. Illinois
23. A bag of nuts
24. Wigan
25. Edinburgh
26. Nick Leeson
27. 3 years old
28. The Kinks
29. Orange
30. Emmeline Pankhurst
31. Diesel Engine Road Vehicle
32. Earth
33. Rubella
34. Jonny Wilkinson
35. Berkshire
36. Suez Canal
37. Tecwen Whittock
38. Columbia
39. Tikrit
40. Sarah Palin

Quiz 11

1. *Life for Rent,* Dido
2. Idi Amin
3. Denis Thatcher
4. HMS *Sheffield*
5. *Mamma Mia*
6. 'When I'm 64'
7. California
8. 118
9. David Blaine
10. Michael Owen
11. Philadelphia
12. A rabbit
13. Alexander Graham Bell
14. Toploader
15. West Bromwich Albion
16. Boots
17. Blackjack
18. The *Sun*
19. Arc de Triomphe
20. False
21. Bones
22. Jim Clark
23. Cancer
24. A puppy
25. Split or divided skirts
26. Asia
27. Pogo dancing, or 'pogoing'
28. Ireland
29. King William IV
30. Digital Audio Tape
31. Augusta
32. The head
33. The Forth Road Bridge
34. Ashford & Simpson
35. Drury Lane
36. Mikhail Gorbachev
37. Mars
38. Thierry Henry
39. China
40. Robert Kilroy Silk

Super-dooper!

Quiz 12

1. On the eye
2. James Hanratty
3. Manic Street Preachers
4. Ayresome Park
5. Edinburgh
6. Crisp
7. Please turn over
8. The Calder
9. 14
10. Vixen
11. Contraceptives
12. L'Oréal
13. It had the highest temperature recorded
    in the UK at 38.5°C (101.3°F)
14. John Coffey
15. Columbus
16. Rubik's cube
17. 'Dizzy'
18. President of the USA
19. Eddie Waring
20. Crimean War
21. Austin
22. A cherry tree
23. Rhodes
24. 'Millennium'
25. Qantas
26. St George
27. Steve Davis
28. Peter Kay
29. Stamp Duty
30. Elizabeth II
31. The Labour Party
32. Detroit
33. John D. Rockefeller
34. Officer Dibble
35. Cathay Pacific
36. 8
37. Bruce Springsteen
38. L. S. Lowry
39. *Full Metal Jacket*
40. Curly Wurly

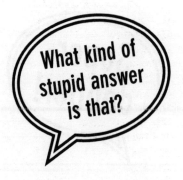
What kind of stupid answer is that?

Quiz 13

1. 1997
2. Decca
3. Pepper
4. The Russians
5. Double Diamond
6. Colorado
7. Rose
8. Marc Bolan
9. Nashville
10. 11 (2 parents, 2 grandparents, 7 children, and 1 cousin in Seasons 3–9)
11. Jack Charlton
12. Ordinary
13. Space
14. Ra-ra skirt
15. Special Weapons and Tactics
16. Seven (I, V, X, L, D, C and M)
17. Neil Ruddock
18. 'Careless Whisper'
19. Electronic
20. Dice
21. Snowy
22. Lime tree
23. Harry S. Truman
24. Kentucky Fried Chicken
25. Emma Noble
26. Bile
27. Kool and the Gang
28. Sony
29. Mo Mowlam
30. Shake 'N' Vac
31. Dead Sea
32. Salt Lake City
33. M25 London Orbital
34. Sale Sharks
35. Road
36. The dock
37. Pawn
38. The Verve
39. Torbay
40. Humidity

Quiz 14

1. Amstel
2. Shamrock
3. Summer Bay
4. They are all fire signs
5. Gold
6. 'Crazy In Love'
7. Toad
8. Texan Bar
9. The Lions
10. Philips
11. *Shameless*
12. Between the Arizona and Nevada state lines, on the Colorado River
13. Watt
14. Gary and Martin Kemp
15. Kent
16. Gossard
17. The Human League
18. Port of Spain
19. Chipper
20. Lime (Harry Lime)
21. Nimbus
22. Paper folding
23. Moscow
24. Janet Jackson
25. It was stolen
26. Walford
27. Cat litter
28. National Express
29. A metre
30. 3
31. Old King Cole
32. Missouri
33. Ben Hogan
34. Fry's Chocolate Cream
35. Liver
36. Jupiter
37. Red
38. Brixton, London
39. The Acid Bath Murderer
40. Prague

Quiz 15

1. *The Royal*
2. 'You've Lost That Loving Feeling'
3. A petrol bomb
4. Blue Lagoon
5. Ian Botham
6. Copper and zinc
7. Hull City
8. New York City
9. Karl Benz
10. Jordan
11. Athens, Greece
12. The Who
13. Elizabeth Arden
14. Florida
15. Pac Man
16. Canada
17. Proctor & Gamble
18. Richard II
19. Pluto
20. Moulin Rouge
21. It indicates World Cup wins
22. Italy
23. The White Sea
24. Mule
25. Budapest
26. David Bowie
27. Silver
28. Aeroflot
29. Tenerife
30. 'SOS' by ABBA
31. *The Beano*
32. George VI
33. Coyote
34. Extremely low temperatures
35. Two
36. Black
37. The miniskirt
38. La Paz, Bolivia
39. Biscuit
40. Perennial

Crikey, what a thicko!

Quiz 16

1. 18
2. 1089
3. Lou Bega
4. Grand Central, New York
5. A murder
6. Swansea
7. Bananarama
8. 170
9. John Travolta
10. The Yen
11. The Baltic Sea
12. Tottenham Hotspur
13. Prince Andrew behind Charles, William and Harry
14. Judas
15. Ray Parker Jnr
16. Power station
17. Dwight Yorke
18. The ear
19. John Reginald Christie
20. Lancaster and York
21. The Nile
22. Chicago
23. Farthing
24. Maine
25. Rick Buckler
26. The bat
27. Blue Hawaii
28. Denmark
29. Volvo
30. New Look
31. Neville Southall
32. Betty Boothroyd
33. 5,000
34. 'Echo Beach'
35. The Old Bailey
36. Boob tube
37. Vincent Vega
38. British Gas privatization
39. Gretna Green
40. Lonnie Donegan

Quiz 17

1. Iced Gems
2. Great Wall of China
3. The first
4. The Eagle
5. Sir Galahad
6. Green Shield Stamps
7. Jimmy Nail
8. Denmark
9. Thursday's
10. Dorothy's dog in *The Wizard of Oz*
11. 31 January 1983
12. Mexican peso
13. The Yorkshire Ripper
14. Steve Harmison
15. David and Ken
16. A draughtsman
17. Condor
18. In the knee
19. Argentina
20. Kent
21. Mary Shelley
22. MS *Herald of Free Enterprise*
23. Rimmel
24. Richard Nixon
25. A tie
26. Austrian
27. Washington DC
28. Jessica Lange
29. X-ray, Yankee and Zulu
30. Honolulu
31. Gibraltar
32. Queen Anne
33. Moscow
34. A fret
35. Points given for a football win
36. The Yangtze
37. Billy Idol
38. Light travels faster than sound
39. Bristol itself is a county
40. A will

Quiz 18

1. Left
2. Pole
3. John Glenn
4. Nicosia
5. William Joyce
6. Kiev
7. *The Dandy*
8. Sweet
9. Michael Owen
10. Dead Sea
11. Catherine Howard
12. Alicante
13. Hock
14. 'Baby One More Time'
15. River Aire
16. Norm
17. The Claret Jug
18. 1053
19. Hot pants
20. −26.1 in Newport, Shropshire
21. Peter Kay
22. £1 coin
23. Bass
24. Hatton Garden
25. Chester-le-Street, County Durham
26. Gwyneth Paltrow
27. Sangatte
28. Hamster
29. The time signal
30. Spanx
31. The Bahamas
32. Kate Winslet
33. Itchycoo Park
34. Abu Dhabi
35. Candles
36. Margaret Thatcher
37. Colin Montgomerie
38. 2
39. Glasses
40. The England World Cup Squad

Quiz 19

1. 3 years
2. Jamie Oliver
3. Poland
4. Secret Squirrel
5. Winston Churchill
6. 6
7. Jane Torvill and Christopher Dean
8. Shaggy
9. Blue
10. Nadine Coyle
11. *Absolutely Fabulous*
12. South Africa
13. Frank Lampard
14. Yasser Arafat
15. Sophie, Countess of Wessex
16. Portsmouth (1939–45)
17. Vitamin D
18. Spain
19. Windsor Castle
20. Florence Griffith – Joyner
21. *Greatest Hits,* Queen
22. Springbok
23. 1955
24. Armada
25. International Date Line
26. Italy
27. Cameron Diaz
28. Ballpoint pen
29. Aylesbury
30. *Billy Elliot*
31. Trevor Francis
32. Tuna fish
33. File Transfer Protocol
34. Royal Mail Group
35. George
36. Venus
37. Sherbet
38. Wimpy
39. Grace Kelly
40. Prince William

Quiz 20

1. Mir
2. Mammals
3. Pound notes
4. Monopoly
5. *Twin Peaks*
6. Libya
7. Argentina
8. Lord Chief Justice
9. Adverts for alcoholic drinks
10. Yorkie
11. 666
12. False – he was born in Cardiff
13. Joe Strummer
14. Bert
15. Lambeth Palace
16. Argon
17. Ibiza
18. Community Service
19. Yorkshire
20. District of Columbia
21. Rafael Nadal
22. Tom Hanks
23. Red
24. 40
25. Albert Einstein
26. 'Sailor'
27. Bar (barrow, barking and barrage)
28. Pandora
29. *The Word*
30. A raven
31. The samba
32. Mexico
33. Kazakhstan
34. Marie Curie
35. New Zealand
36. Sainsbury's
37. Post script
38. *Playschool*
39. 257
40. Tallahassee

Quiz 21

1. PlayStation
2. Sandy Lyle
3. Iran
4. Jane Fonda
5. John Roberts
6. *Crackerjack*
7. Dozens
8. Bridge
9. Mount Teide, Tenerife
10. *Only Fools And Horses*
11. Liverpool
12. The motorcycle
13. Sole
14. Rihanna
15. Nigel Mansell
16. She won a million on *Who Wants to Be a Millionaire?*
17. Hippopotamus
18. Florence Nightingale
19. Volt(s)
20. Mr Tickle
21. J. Edgar Hoover
22. Walford East
23. Santa Cruz
24. Germany
25. Jeremy Vine
26. Red and yellow cards
27. Boy George
28. Vote
29. Lulu
30. Orange
31. A pen
32. Party
33. 5
34. Brazil
35. Essex
36. Terrier
37. 13 years old
38. Centrica
39. Cameron Diaz
40. The Rembrandts

Quiz 22

1. Chris Moyles
2. The kitchen
3. Gin
4. Infernal
5. Derby County
6. Ottawa
7. America only had 13 states when it was founded
8. Ultrasound
9. The Porsche 911
10. Half past 10
11. The liver
12. Green
13. Boxing
14. English Civil War
15. George Best
16. Tamagotchi
17. Blue Mink
18. Glenn Close
19. Sow
20. France
21. Neptune
22. Czech Republic
23. Commander
24. A hamlet
25. Yellow
26. Blue
27. Morrisons
28. Blackcurrant
29. Volkswagen
30. Emma Thompson
31. March
32. The Penny Black
33. A shark
34. Rimmel
35. Tupac Shakur
36. Pony
37. Apple
38. Norfolk
39. Richard Gere
40. Cathode

Quiz 23

1. The Loire
2. Exosphere
3. Almonds
4. A million
5. Manslaughter
6. Three
7. Glasgow
8. 12 years old
9. *Mork & Mindy*
10. A clef
11. Sir Winston Churchill
12. Drams
13. Robert the Bruce
14. Bogotá
15. Topshop
16. Light Emitting Diode
17. Black Eyed Peas
18. Golf
19. *Boogie Nights*
20. A wraparound skirt
21. Hummingbird
22. Nike
23. Carrying out hangings
24. Violet
25. Alan B'stard
26. Snow
27. Indonesia
28. Ronald Reagan
29. Louise Redknapp (née Nurding)
30. Alcohol
31. Indiana Jones
32. London Bridge
33. Electricity
34. Wraps stone
35. Pudsey
36. Gardening
37. 50
38. Tin and lead
39. Janus
40. Brown

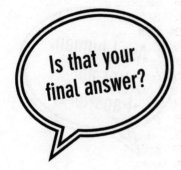

Is that your final answer?

Quiz 24

1. Gerry and the Pacemakers
2. Valletta
3. Liverpool
4. Uniform
5. A duck
6. Yellow and purple
7. 1951
8. It has used up fuel
9. Ralph Lauren
10. Battle of Bosworth
11. Kevin
12. Strawberry
13. World War I
14. Music
15. *Dick and Dom In Da Bungalow*
16. WRNS (Women's Royal Naval Service)
17. Arsenic
18. Herring
19. Newark
20. Special Brew
21. Albumen
22. John Malkovich
23. *The* (*Daily*) *Mirror*
24. £100
25. The Tawe
26. Franklin D. Roosevelt
27. Damon Hill
28. Standard Trunk Dialling
29. Cheese
30. Tanzania
31. *Spitting Image*
32. E
33. Duncan Fletcher
34. Iran
35. BBC Broadcasting House
36. Overlord
37. London City Airport
38. Roger Moore (7 times)
39. Olympia
40. A fish

Quiz 25

1. Red
2. REO Speedwagon
3. Wonderbra
4. Windscale
5. Tulle
6. British Columbia
7. None (it was Noah who built the Ark)
8. 1971
9. A stingray
10. World Wide Web
11. William Roach
12. A dog (terrier)
13. Carbon monoxide
14. Tailoring
15. US Masters
16. *Live and Kicking*
17. World War I
18. West to Bristol
19. Lewis Hamilton
20. 4.5
21. Uranus
22. Inspiral Carpets
23. *Watership Down*
24. A stallion
25. A person who drives sheep or cattle
26. Dime
27. One
28. Lord Louis Mountbatten
29. Lycra
30. Flying
31. Purple
32. Cornwall
33. Laughing gas
34. Scotland
35. Scott Tracy
36. Mixture of metals
37. 1953
38. Dartmouth (Devon)
39. Epsilon
40. Ankara

Quiz 26

1. Newton and Ridley
2. The Move
3. Kohl
4. Oxygen
5. Footpath
6. Dave Gilmour
7. China
8. Muhammad Ali
9. Fireman Sam
10. Sturgeon
11. San Francisco
12. Diners Club
13. Sir Isaac Pitman
14. Gerry Adams
15. Bullseye
16. The banana
17. Ronan Keating
18. Marco Polo
19. William Gladstone
20. Cuba
21. Paddington bear
22. Blue, Yellow, Black, Green and Red
23. Give Way
24. Toronto
25. 42
26. St George's Cross
27. Breakdance
28. Guinness
29. Steve Brookstein
30. Thomas Crapper
31. M8
32. Fulham (established 1879)
33. 12
34. Champagne and peach juice
35. The Danube
36. *EastEnders*
37. Nailcare products
38. *King Rollo*
39. Horses
40. USA

Quiz 27

1. House of Commons
2. Spanish
3. Cain
4. The Old Lady of Threadneedle Street
5. Pluto
6. Michael Collins
7. The Kinks
8. Tony Adams (born 10 October 1966)
9. A spat
10. Ecuador
11. Levi Strauss
12. The Red Sea
13. Ginger beer
14. A
15. Post Office Protocol
16. *The Muppet Show*
17. 1954
18. Lettuce
19. 36
20. 150 knots
21. Phil Collins
22. Uranus
23. Discovery
24. Mandy Pandy
25. Edinburgh
26. White
27. Leeds Rhinos
28. Leon Trotsky
29. DCI Gene Hunt
30. 4 – Newcastle (twice), Fulham, England and Manchester City
31. Copyright
32. Shoes
33. Rednex
34. Lech Walesa
35. River Clyde
36. *James and the Giant Peach*
37. Pretty Polly
38. The flux capacitor
39. Between its ears
40. 6

Quiz 28

1. Singapore
2. Traction Control System
3. Stereophonics
4. Mercury
5. Glasgow
6. *Never Say Never Again*
7. Pole vaulting
8. Nationwide
9. Mike Reid
10. Honeybee
11. 57 (the others are prime numbers)
12. A dwarf
13. Nevada
14. A medium-sized boiled egg
15. Because he's not dead
16. M60
17. 50 years
18. Alfred Hitchcock
19. Pennsylvania
20. Procter & Gamble
21. Celtic Manor Resort in Newport, Wales
22. Razorlight
23. B, C, M and P
24. Wayne Mark Rooney
25. The Leeds Studios
26. They all lie near the foot of a volcano
27. Playtex
28. Michael Palin
29. Reykjavik
30. Shark
31. North Carolina, South Carolina, North Dakota and South Dakota
32. Socks
33. Ambridge
34. Ricotta
35. An aglet
36. David Jason
37. Francis Ford Coppola
38. 121
39. The ionosphere
40. File transfer protocol

Quiz 29

1. Bingo, Drooper, Fleegle and Snorky
2. Radiohead
3. A gaggle
4. Large Hadron Collider
5. Hansie Cronje
6. River Main
7. 8 hours behind
8. *The X Factor*
9. Sugar
10. Pat Benatar
11. The iris
12. GB (Gordon Brown)
13. 2000
14. *Top Cat*
15. 42
16. Widnes
17. A squirrel
18. Arizona
19. Mercury
20. His Master's Voice
21. Viper and Jester
22. Bobby Sands
23. Clarence Birdseye
24. Duran Duran
25. Royal flush
26. Soviet Union
27. *Reservoir Dogs*
28. They are both nicknamed The Tigers
29. *Grange Hill*
30. Traffic wardens
31. Abu Ghraib
32. Perth
33. Gwen Stefani
34. A flower
35. Gordon the Gopher
36. True
37. Los Angeles
38. Boeing Aircraft Corporation
39. J. R. Hartley
40. Bobby and Jack Charlton

Don't forget, even if the answer sounds wrong, it's not!

Quiz 30

1. Henry I
2. Bob Monkhouse
3. Pink
4. Spiders
5. Kate Lawler
6. Cuba
7. USA
8. Brass
9. The equator runs through them
10. *The Liver Birds*
11. Knightsbridge
12. The Quakers
13. Flora
14. Moxey
15. *Lady Chatterley's Lover*
16. Cumbria
17. Snake
18. George Michael
19. One (the moon)
20. Show jumping
21. Dreamt
22. 4
23. Newcastle Brown Ale
24. Brian Cant
25. Tower of London
26. M
27. Max Factor
28. They have won the FA Cup
29. A brood
30. Magna Carta
31. Channel Five
32. Red
33. Beehive
34. 18
35. Emley Moor Mast
36. *Viz*
37. 100
38. Neil Kinnock
39. Bad Attitude
40. Humerus

Quiz 31

1. 25 years old
2. Leeds School of Medicine
3. 6 (5 short and 1 long)
4. Stephanie Mangano
5. Green
6. Newquay
7. Cats
8. Kevin Pietersen
9. Sicily
10. Omega
11. Speed Buggy
12. The Olympic Games
13. The Vapors
14. Canard
15. In the heel
16. Bolívar
17. River Ribble
18. *Hollyoaks*
19. Michael Jackson
20. Denmark's
21. Wigan Athletic
22. Cheryl Cole
23. 1,000
24. True
25. Mulberry
26. Tripoli
27. Oxygen
28. Bruce Willis
29. Links course
30. Red
31. Genesis
32. *Rainbow*
33. Stansted
34. A heifer
35. 3
36. 27 (10 Commandments + 7 Sacraments + 7 deadly sins + 3 Holy Trinity)
37. Prince
38. Houston
39. Silence of the Lambs
40. Helium (he), nitrogen (n) and sodium (na)

Quiz 32

1. Ibiza
2. Tina Teaspoon
3. Moths
4. Gucci
5. Isobar
6. *Super Bowl XXX*
7. Vostok 1
8. South Africa
9. Terry McCann
10. He was stabbed with a umbrella laced with ricin
11. Opening on a Sunday
12. Metronome
13. Dynamite
14. Cupcakes
15. False
16. John Sullivan
17. A salary
18. Venus
19. Maverick Records
20. Renée Zellweger
21. Mali
22. GG
23. 13
24. Dusty Springfield
25. Pingu
26. 29.5
27. Bonn
28. South Africa
29. Robinsons
30. Bakery
31. Ringo Starr
32. Indian Ocean
33. Ten
34. Abraham Lincoln
35. Alcatraz
36. John Constable
37. John McCarthy
38. *Inch High, Private Eye*
39. High Street
40. The Open University

Quiz 33

1. *Alien Autopsy*
2. Typewriter
3. None
4. 1985
5. Goodison Park (Everton)
6. Luciano Pavarotti
7. Eight
8. Italy's main stock exchange
9. *Brothers in Arms* by Dire Straits
10. Dambusters
11. 5 (*Goldfinger, Thunderball, Moonraker, Octopussy* and *Goldeneye*)
12. When it is flown on a ship
13. China
14. 25 mph
15. Heikki Kovalainen
16. Brazil, Colombia and Ecuador
17. *Fraggle Rock*
18. Kelly's eye
19. Autobahn
20. True
21. Cyril 'Blakey' Blake
22. St David
23. The Stone Roses
24. November
25. Run a mile
26. The Tower of London
27. Spot
28. The Deputy Speaker
29. Epsom Derby
30. *West Side Story*
31. Sheep
32. Empire State Building
33. Body mass index
34. Crown
35. Lord Kitchener
36. Matador
37. Portsmouth
38. Uniform Resource Locator
39. Basement Jaxx
40. Lionel Ritchie

Quiz 34

1. Beirut
2. Soda water
3. Mike Tyson
4. Horatio Nelson
5. Keyboard/typewriter
6. Burt Reynolds
7. Montreal
8. Starburst
9. 16th century
10. Spanish
11. Daffyd Thomas
12. 10
13. Paul Anka
14. M6
15. Sagittarius
16. Wellington boots
17. Mahjong
18. Skylab
19. Russia
20. Luton Town
21. The US stock market
22. Basketball
23. *Only Fools and Horses*
24. 'Up Where We Belong'
25. The bikini
26. *Cheers*
27. Edward J. Smith
28. A performance of 'All You Need Is Love' by The Beatles
29. Donington Park
30. Shoes
31. Homer Simpson
32. Bryan Ferry
33. Bernhard Langer
34. Acid
35. Jeff Wayne
36. The *Daily Telegraph*
37. Boys from the Blackstuff
38. Bakewell
39. Eric Cantona (in August, 1992)
40. 7

Quiz 35

1. Cognac
2. Peter Andre
3. 1964
4. The Thrills
5. June
6. Hang Seng
7. Wedge-shaped
8. Hedge Sparrow
9. *Family Fortunes*
10. Miami
11. 'It's My Life'
12. Bourbon
13. Lawn Tennis Association
14. Mansion House
15. Venus
16. Edward III
17. Semtex
18. The wink
19. *Last of the Summer Wine*
20. Glasgow
21. Duran Duran
22. Woolsack
23. Yellow
24. The atomic bombs that fell on Japan
25. South Korea
26. 'Be prepared'
27. Weed
28. Stella
29. 36 dollars
30. Arsenal, Blackburn, Chelsea and Manchester United
31. Yahoo
32. Russell Brand
33. A rolling stone gathers no moss
34. 'All Shook Up'
35. High blood pressure
36. UN Secretary General
37. Ian Beale (Adam Woodyatt)
38. Spain
39. True
40. 300

I'm the Archbishop of answers, baby!

Quiz 36

1. Dead Sea
2. £1 coin
3. Ringo Starr
4. Goodwood, Plumpton, Ludlow and Huntingdon
5. Edinburgh
6. Keeley Hawes
7. Intelligence
8. Bono
9. Barnsley
10. It was the last Apollo mission
11. Walmart
12. La Paz
13. Chatsworth Estate
14. Bank
15. Loons
16. Peterborough United and Reading
17. Lemon and melon
18. Jack and George
19. Tupperware party
20. Star City
21. Davina McCall
22. Roulette
23. England (Stockton & Darlington Railway)
24. The Internet
25. 9,550 years old
26. 1990
27. *America's Most Wanted*
28. J
29. Fawn
30. Kent
31. Gap
32. The Hudson River
33. Desert Storm
34. Kings of Leon
35. 50 miles
36. *The Lion King*
37. I
38. Electric current
39. Battle of Britain
40. Manila

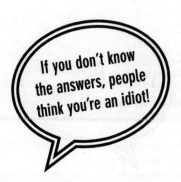

If you don't know the answers, people think you're an idiot!

Quiz 37

1. Bristol
2. A guitar
3. The London Eye
4. Italy
5. Black and white (the colours of the jackets on the dogs in greyhound racing)
6. 'Another Brick In The Wall'
7. *The Dandy*
8. *Sex and the City*
9. Bullseye
10. Polyvinyl chloride
11. Empty tomb
12. Guinness
13. A baby's dummy
14. Aries
15. 53
16. Africa
17. Chris Evans and Gaby Roslin
18. 'Wannabe'
19. Joe Mercer
20. Birdwatching
21. On the left
22. Mars
23. John Lennon
24. Cinzano
25. 28
26. Vauxhall
27. *Rainbow Warrior*
28. Oxford
29. Grace
30. Stealth Bomber
31. 1936
32. Hill Valley
33. The British Empire
34. *Britain's Got Talent*
35. Ho Chi Minh City
36. The Wailers
37. Elephant
38. Gary Lineker
39. Hawaii
40. Napoleon Bonaparte

Quiz 38

1. *The Millennium Falcon*
2. 3
3. Fish
4. Leonardo Da Vinci
5. Mont Blanc
6. Trams
7. Kelly Jones
8. Apollo 11
9. A skirt
10. The eyes
11. Coffee
12. A drum
13. Liverpool
14. Eczema
15. *Family Guy*
16. £10 (a 'tenor')
17. Montpelier
18. Anders Celsius
19. Space bar
20. Jeremy Irons
21. 8 (opposite sides on a clock face)
22. On the moon
23. The Yamuna, or Jumna
24. A trunk
25. Paul Potts
26. France, Spain and Morocco
27. Tomato
28. Hearts, Peterhead and Brechin
29. Tokyo
30. Chris Patten
31. 4
32. Renault
33. Bananarama
34. Palindrome
35. Static electricity
36. Vanilla, chocolate and strawberry
37. *Byker Grove*
38. Lufthansa
39. Afghanistan and Pakistan
40. 3

Quiz 39

1. Ireland
2. *Steptoe and Son*
3. Lance Armstrong
4. Mauritius
5. Gordon Ramsey
6. A queen
7. 'Anarchy in the UK'
8. Green, white and red
9. St Paul's
10. Newcastle United
11. New Zealand
12. M20
13. Martin Scorsese
14. Rapid Eye Movement
15. 1994
16. *Emmerdale*
17. Jamiroquai
18. The Book of Numbers
19. True
20. £60
21. Oxford
22. Shropshire
23. Manchester
24. River Avon
25. A clock
26. -40
27. Milton Keynes
28. Corn
29. Berry Gordy
30. Rome
31. *Monty Python's Flying Circus*
32. Erwin Rommel
33. Multimedia Messaging Service
34. Turtles
35. *The Black Pig*
36. Enola Gay
37. Inverness
38. Margarita
39. Darren Gough
40. Moloko

Quiz 40

1. Sherri and Terri
2. Mercury
3. Accra
4. A skirt
5. Peterborough
6. 0
7. Richard Attenborough
8. Backstreet Boys
9. Kenya
10. Granada Television
11. USA, China and Japan
12. Captain Flack and Pugh, Pugh, Barney McGrew, Cuthbert, Dibble and Grubb
13. Straw-weight
14. Wookie
15. *Little Britain*
16. Gobi
17. Colon
18. Connie Booth
19. Birmingham
20. True
21. 12 (clockwise numbers on a dartboard)
22. U2
23. Direct from a corner kick
24. Portugal
25. 22
26. A black cap
27. Henry VIII
28. Grapes
29. United Kingdom
30. Vauxhall
31. Schmeichel
32. 'Freedom'
33. Transistors
34. 4
35. Kentucky
36. Tweety Pie
37. A four-bagger
38. Queen Victoria
39. Crystal Palace
40. Boot

Quiz 41

1. Kaiser Chiefs
2. One ninth
3. A puffin
4. Mother-in-law
5. Sulphuric acid
6. *Moonraker*
7. Smog
8. *Issues*
9. Peter Shilton
10. Blusher
11. Computer-Aided Design
12. Popeye
13. Métro
14. T Rex
15. John Major
16. *Spycatcher*
17. Frank Whittle
18. Lighter
19. The North Sea
20. The Boo Radleys
21. India
22. Cornetto
23. 6
24. 9 ¾
25. The Boer War
26. 6 (Dopey was the only one not to have one)
27. 5 ft 8 in (1.73m)
28. 'Unfinished' Symphony
29. In a car engine
30. Earth
31. Fortissimo; very loud
32. Clarissa Dickson Wright and Jennifer Paterson
33. Air pressure
34. Helsinki
35. 1934
36. Mia Wallace
37. 90 years
38. Nucleus
39. Nassau
40. The General Lee

Ummmm, nice scores!

Quiz 42

1. Yorkshire
2. Canada
3. Sri Lanka
4. Zagreb
5. *Men Behaving Badly*
6. Skirt lengths
7. The Crimean War
8. *Desperate Housewives*
9. Halibut
10. Christopher Columbus
11. William Pitt the Younger
12. AC/DC
13. Kate Winslet
14. Laszlo Biro
15. Heather Mills
16. Rumpelstiltskin
17. Central Intelligence Agency
18. India
19. Michelle Pfeiffer
20. Alan Shearer and Adrian Chiles
21. Cuba
22. Pluto
23. Any colour
24. Inland Revenue
25. Inner ear
26. Buffalo Bill
27. Jasper Carrott
28. Seventies
29. *The Banana Splits Adventure Hour*
30. Ireland
31. Tuesday
32. Apple
33. No English manager has won
    the Premier League
34. An auctioneer
35. Red
36. 6
37. The Nags Head
38. Alaska
39. A welder
40. A rook

Quiz 43

1. Take That
2. Fred Trueman
3. Northallerton
4. Richard Nixon
5. Mark Chapman
6. Inspector Gadget
7. Egg whites
8. Bryan Robson
9. Japan
10. Geometry
11. Mumbai
12. Gary Lineker
13. Silicon
14. Sugar
15. Joe Calzaghe
16. Midge Ure
17. Platform
18. Taurus
19. She was the girl in the BBC's test card
20. Lizardfish
21. Manque
22. Norway
23. Under a skirt or dress
24. Australia
25. They were robots
26. *Paint Your Wagon*
27. Man overboard
28. North Pole
29. Cu
30. Market Rasen, Lincolnshire
31. The Thrills
32. Bananaman
33. Eight
34. A chick
35. Kylie Minogue
36. The Tower of London
37. Rio de Janeiro
38. Andy Murray
39. Jamie Theakston
40. I

Quiz 44

1. £250,000
2. 3 minutes
3. Crossed swords
4. Bakers
5. The Tiber
6. Mars
7. *American Idol*
8. Dash Dash Dash
9. Akela
10. Ropes
11. Tom Baker
12. University of Leeds and Leeds Metropolitan University
13. Prince Harry
14. India
15. Canter
16. Roman Abramovich
17. Roll Deep
18. Zambesi
19. 10
20. The Lovell Radio Telescope
21. Anne Frank
22. The rat
23. Tottenham Hotspur
24. Steve Irwin
25. Christian Louboutin
26. Level 42
27. Henrik Larsson
28. *Neighbours*
29. The time in the UK read as 01:02:03 04.05.06
30. Bulgaria
31. Queen Elizabeth 1
32. *Loose Women*
33. New York City
34. Oliver Cromwell
35. Her left leg
36. Potatoes
37. *Definitely Maybe*
38. A, B, O, and AB
39. Red and white
40. Margaret Roberts

Quiz 45

1. Bungle
2. Southampton
3. White European
4. Rasputin
5. Arthur Lowe
6. Nicolas Anelka (7 transfers, £85 million)
7. Morning
8. Ayers Rock
9. Hale-Bopp
10. Hillary Clinton
11. Valerie
12. 1¾ pints
13. Edinburgh
14. They were all Grand National-winning horses
15. Dizzy
16. *The Royle Family*
17. Robbie Williams
18. Oxford Circus
19. Eric Bristow
20. *Toy Story*
21. Cairo
22. Belgium
23. ABBA
24. Anthony Blunt
25. *The Fast Show*
26. 1955
27. Vitamin C
28. *Backbeat*
29. Headingley
30. 12
31. Sydney Harbour Bridge
32. Tortoise
33. Hourglass
34. Daniel Bedingfield
35. Cooperman
36. The Great Fire of London
37. Steve Strange and Boy George
38. *Coronation Street*
39. Ag
40. Laura Ashley

Quiz 46

1. France
2. 1,411
3. Queens Park Rangers
4. Pacific Ocean
5. Australia
6. Jessica Rabbit
7. Mascara
8. Trumpet, tuba, trombone and horn
9. Riga
10. Yasser Arafat
11. Silver
12. Guardian Angels
13. Karl Benz
14. The liver
15. Zack Mayo
16. Sheffield
17. The feet
18. White
19. 88 mph
20. Glenn Hoddle
21. Pearl Harbor
22. Wikipedia
23. Dung beetle
24. *Celebrity Big Brother*
25. River Irwell
26. Kim Cattrall
27. 4 shots under par
28. Stiletto
29. Woodwind
30. Mikhail Gorbachev
31. Nebraska
32. Carrie Fisher
33. 20
34. Red Hot Chili Peppers
35. The North Sea
36. Aquarius
37. Tin
38. Cambridge
39. Holly Willoughby
40. True

Quiz 47

1. Ronald Reagan and Konstantin Chernenko
2. Giraffe
3. Princess Margaret
4. Mr Jinx
5. Neville Chamberlain
6. Theodore Roosevelt
7. Didier Drogba
8. Three-day week
9. *Carousel*
10. River Trent
11. 'Country House'
12. The Ghostbusters
13. Nigel Lawson
14. Ingrid Bergman
15. A cat
16. Seahorse
17. Pepsi
18. Maine
19. *Friends*
20. Pink
21. George III
22. Mon Mome
23. *The Dandy*
24. Ernie Els (won in 2002 and lost in 2004)
25. Lyon
26. Diamond
27. 19th century
28. Carly Simon
29. 12 years
30. Sixteen
31. A poodle skirt
32. C
33. Penelope Pitstop
34. The Rio Grande
35. Pine nuts
36. Horseracing
37. Oasis
38. *Life for Rent*
39. A calf
40. 225

It's only easy if you know the answers

Quiz 48

1. E
2. Goldie Hawn
3. Boeing 777
4. Lactose
5. Zurich
6. Dave
7. Green
8. Admiral of the Fleet
9. Michael Sheen
10. 500
11. Mascara
12. England
13. Pet Shop Boys
14. Chopper
15. 7
16. Ronnie Barker
17. Eros
18. 'Garden Gate' or 'One Fat Lady'
19. A rook
20. Tallahassee
21. Rubber
22. U2
23. Renault
24. 12
25. Jeremy Clarkson
26. On the back of a £10 note
27. 50 Cent
28. Tom
29. United Kingdom
30. Bill Clinton
31. Local Area Network
32. Ballroom
33. 1984
34. 155
35. 617
36. A marinated herring
37. Nicole Kidman
38. 2 fish and 5 loaves
39. The leek
40. Culture Club

That's it, knowledge jousters

Quiz 49

1. 144
2. Joe Wright
3. Sperm whale
4. The 02
5. She was arrested for allowing her pupils to name a teddy bear Muhammed
6. 1 July 2007
7. Australia
8. 'Grace Kelly' by Mika
9. Boris Yeltsin
10. River Don
11. 3
12. Tony Blair
13. *Harry Potter and the Deathly Hallows*
14. Chic
15. Brazil
16. Kevin Greening
17. Salman Rushdie
18. She was caught driving while banned
19. India
20. Texas
21. Fabio Capello
22. Topshop
23. Whitehaven
24. 2001
25. Queue
26. 815
27. One stroke is added to the score
28. Marble
29. Catatonia
30. 10
31. Joe Calzaghe
32. Nowhere (a London bus runs on diesel)
33. Anita Roddick
34. David Beckham
35. Blofeld
36. Houses of Parliament
37. Texas
38. USA, France, Japan and Hong Kong
39. Leeds
40. 20/20 (Twenty20 cricket)

Quiz 50

1. Norwich
2. 216
3. Bullseye
4. Dennis Waterman
5. Mount St Helens
6. Cuba
7. Corner Shop
8. 5
9. Oklahoma City
10. St James' Park
11. A= 13 B = 7 C = 20
12. Keiren Fallon
13. 15
14. Bucephalus (Ox-head)
15. Buckingham Palace
16. His body
17. Fossils
18. Edinburgh
19. Do not bleach
20. American Airlines
21. Chelsea in 2000 and 2007
22. Wilson Pickett
23. Exocet
24. Kellogg's Cornflakes
25. Hard black
26. Sega
27. Elisha Otis
28. Hard disk drive
29. Barney Rubble
30. Moses
31. Michelin
32. Kenny Everett
33. The North Pole
34. 16
35. *Thriller*
36. Christian Dior
37. Jerusalem
38. Floyd Mayweather Jr
39. Heroine
40. 1984